ADVANCE PRAISE FOR

What good work Frank Cunningham has done with *Vesper Time*. His underlying thesis that growing old is a way of prayer is quite wonderful. We're about the same age and I'm trying to see it that way myself. His book is an invitation to more fully engage this stage of our journey and be enriched by it.

RICHARD ROHR

CENTER FOR ACTION AND CONTEMPLATION

Vesper Time is a book full of wisdom and guidance for all who want to treat aging as "a school of the spirit"—a time to call upon the sacred alchemy that turns weakness into strength, loss into gratitude, and dying into new life. Wonderfully well-written, grounded in real-life experience, and infused with Frank Cunningham's "sacramental imagination," this book about aging with grace is, in fact, a book for all seasons.

PARKER J. PALMER

AUTHOR, *LET YOUR LIFE SPEAK, A HIDDEN WHOLENESS,*
AND *HEALING THE HEART OF DEMOCRACY*

Anyone who has gazed at the rising moon or the emerging stars at twilight knows the beauty of this hour of day. Frank Cunningham reminds us that the *Vesper Time* of life is a rich seedbed for spiritual growth. His intimate and engaging chronicle gives voice to the wisdom and pleasures of this time. For those of us who have not yet reached a certain age, but hope to, Cunningham reassures us of the powerful spiritual adventure that awaits.

JUDITH VALENTE

PBS-TV AND WGLT RADIO

AUTHOR, *ATCHISON BLUE* AND *THE ART OF PAUSING*

Vesper Time reminds me of the gentle wisdom of Henri Nouwen's *Genesee Diary*. Both authors have the gift of discretion. They share enough of themselves to identify with their journey in a way that puts the focus on the reader rather than on themselves. Reading *Vesper Time* is like taking a long walk with a wise but down to earth friend. Relax with this book. It will nourish your tired soul.

ROBERT J. WICKS
AUTHOR, *RIDING THE DRAGON*
GENERAL EDITOR, *PRAYER IN THE CATHOLIC TRADITION*

Vesper Time—"evening prayer at the time of the lighting of the lamps, just before darkness descends"—is Frank Cunningham's profound metaphor for spirituality of aging. He shares lamplight for our own Vesper Time with engaging reflections on his life interwoven with illumination from an amazing array of other travelers of the human journey from Cicero to Teillard de Chardin. His insights and practical suggestions inspire us to create a spiritual practice to light the dusk of our own aging.

PATRICIA LIVINGSTON
AUTHOR OF *LESSONS OF THE HEART* AND *THIS BLESSED MESS*

VESPER TIME

*V*ESPER TIME

The Spiritual Practice
of Growing Older

Frank J. Cunningham

ORBIS BOOKS
Maryknoll, New York 10545

ORBIS BOOKS
Maryknoll, New York 10545

Fathers and Brothers
MARYKNOLL™

Sixth Printing, October 2017

Founded in 1970, Orbis Books endeavors to publish works that enlighten the mind, nourish the spirit, and challenge the conscience. The publishing arm of the Maryknoll Fathers and Brothers, Orbis seeks to explore the global dimensions of the Christian faith and mission, to invite dialogue with diverse cultures and religious traditions, and to serve the cause of reconciliation and peace. The books published reflect the views of their authors and do not represent the official position of the Maryknoll Society. To learn more about Maryknoll and Orbis Books, please visit our website at www.maryknollsociety.org.

Manufactured in the United States of America.

Manuscript editing and typesetting by Joan Weber Laflamme.

Library of Congress Cataloging-in-Publication Data

Names: Cunningham, Frank J., author.
Title: Vesper time : the spiritual practice of growing older / Frank J.
    Cunningham ; foreword by Joyce Rupp.
Description: Maryknoll : Orbis Books, 2017.
Identifiers: LCCN 2016032706 (print) | LCCN 2016045474 (ebook) |
    ISBN 9781626982314 (pbk.) | ISBN 9781608336968 (ebook)
Subjects: LCSH: Aging—Religious aspects—Catholic Church. | Older
    Christians—Religious life.
Classification: LCC BV4580 .C78 2017 (print) | LCC BV4580 (ebook) |
    DDC 248.8/5—dc23
LC record available at https://lccn.loc.gov/2016032706

For Sue
my breath as I grow old

Contents

Acknowledgments

Thanks to Joyce Rupp, Keith Clark, Gene Hemerick, Bob Wickes, Pat Livingston, Lock Sofield, Bill Breault, Dolores Leckey, Kathy Chesto—writers all. They listened to life, shared their lessons, and coached their coach. Thanks also to Bill Barry for encouraging the possibilities and to Judith Valente, whose invitation to speak resulted in this book.

Portions of this material have appeared in *America, Notre Dame Magazine*, and *US Catholic*.

Foreword

By Joyce Rupp

My life as a published author began when Frank Cunningham took the risk to accept my first book for publication thirty one years ago. I will always carry immense gratitude for his belief in my writing when I barely believed in it myself. Now, these many years later as Frank enters into his elderhood, I have the privilege of writing about the depth and clarity with which he articulates the evolution and maturation of his interior and exterior life.

I've read numerous publications on aging. Most have relevance. Some are ponderous. Few have held my avid interest to the last chapter. *Vesper Time* moves along smoothly, like a pontoon gliding on a flowing river of wisdom. In reading this fine presentation on the later years of life, there was never any thought of pulling up to shore and getting out of the boat until I arrived at the very end of the ride.

What joy to find an approach to aging as balanced, openhearted, and insightful as this one. Frank refers to himself as a "wordsmith" and, indeed, he is. I found this early on when he describes the spiritual practice of aging as "listening to what our lives have to tell us, sifting out the chaff, watching for that quick glint of flame, and clinging to what has nurtured our growth."

Along with the steady movement and creative exploration of the content, his metaphors and comprehensive perceptiveness run deep and wide. He takes us to places of the mind and heart that we might not speak about to others, yet are keenly aware of when another uninvited piece of aging makes a home in us.

Frank notes early in the book, "To examine our story is to embark on a journey inward." *Vesper Time* is much more than an autobiographical accounting of how one arrives at the stage of being an elder. The search for meaning, for a more complete understanding of self and an exploration of personal belief, fills the pages with a clear revelation of how it is to be in the senior years.

You won't find statistics on gerontology and external data on demographics here. Instead you'll travel with the author in exploring aspects of aging gleaned from his own life, as well as from a wide variety of literary and religious sources that confirm and affirm his valuable insights. You will find yourself asking similar questions that his journey has led him to ask, such as "How can diminishment inform my spiritual practice of aging?"

The pages fill with stories and anecdotes, each one revealing, connecting, enhancing, detailing what growing older evokes and requires. This is Frank's story, but it is also the story of all of us who embark on the final decades. His musings, satisfactions, discoveries, acceptances, doubts, and hesitations are ours as well. The de tails may differ but the underlying reality of this ripening stage of life rings true.

I am reminded of Kathleen Dowling Singh's comment in *The Grace of Aging:* "In a beautiful synergy, the telling of the stories, the healing of the wounds, and the letting go of the stories work together to release the teller of the tales." This is what I have observed in *Vesper Time.* Frank states it well: "Aging is about living into our memories, about seeking their meaning, about accepting and being kind to them."

Frank reminds us and shows how the divine is present in the midst of these stories. I especially appreciate his honesty and his willingness to be vulnerable with what he shares. He acknowledges the diminishment that steals one's good health and robs self of the built-in purpose one formerly had in an active career, the need for greater patience, the memory glitches and other aspects of the elder years that slip in unpredicted. He also refers to "rough marital cycles," illness and death of friends, difficult decisions, and his underlying questions regarding faith.

At the same time Frank's approach carries a positive message. He looks for where the treasures can be mined. As he delineates the five leitmotifs of aging he defined for himself and the presentations he gives on aging, the reader is invited to accompany him in seeking greater meaning and fuller peace.

His refreshing humor peppers the pages. Time and again I chuckled at Frank's ability to laugh at his own foibles. I found myself smiling in recognition, nodding my head in kinship, and marking pages where I noted mutual understanding from parallel experiences. I also resonated with the exquisite moments of spiritual intimacy that he allows the reader to witness. Numerous pieces in this book captured my heart—a surprise communing with a buck deer on a daily walk, his last words to his dying mother, a grandchild's "I love you," and his answer to the stirring question "Are you holding me, Lord?"

"Spirituality," Frank notes, "embraces our lives at all levels" and "deals with the dynamics of the heart." *Vesper Time* explores this spirituality with a humble ambiance. There's no touting of ego, no claim to have the magic answers or exceptional religious experiences.

A consistent theme of faithfulness to spiritual growth and personal integrity abounds. Frank describes his

faith as "a nomadic experience . . . far removed from
my youth. . . . I find comfort in my doubt, knowing
it enriches my faith. . . . Certitude troubles me while
mystery enchants." He refers to himself as "a piously
impaired man." Perhaps when it comes to traditional
prayer, but certainly not when his awareness, musings,
and perceptions take on the quality of spun gold, which
they often do in this rendering of elderhood.

Frank finds the holy in the ordinary. Sees it laden
in each part of his life. You won't find some ethereal,
mystifying substance unrelated to daily life as he muses
on the societal and religious turnings and the effect they
have had on his spirituality. Quite the opposite. Frank
encourages paying attention to each part of personal
history, to what it might be revealing about one's hunger
for the Holy.

The reader also receives some challenges regarding
the aging years. Frank suggests that growing in intimacy,
taking risks, being vulnerable, engaging in new experiences, and making our knowledge and skills available in
the service of others are essential if one is to age well.

If I were to summarize this reflective, refreshing book
on the spiritual practice of aging I would use a quote
from the artist Mary Southard. One of her exquisite
paintings is titled "From the arms of love—to the Arms
of Love—Love will keep us." That is the underlying
message Frank Cunningham generously shares with the

reader—an intimate view of his life's journey from a spiritual view. But the focus is never just on himself.

We, the readers, have the opportunity and joy of observing the wisdom he gleaned from his life experiences and brings into the aging process. In doing so, we gain inspiration and courage to enter our own life's journey. From the arms of the Beloved One to the mystery of our returning, we trust—as Frank Cunningham has done— that Love will keep us along the way.

Introduction

In writing this book I hope to stimulate some thought about a couple of questions. The first is: Can we take a step beyond the spirituality of aging and ask if the experience of aging in itself can be a spiritual exercise? The second is: If so, how do we awaken to the experience?

To help the reader engage the questions, I offer reflections on why I think aging is a spiritual exercise and how I have engaged it. Or better yet, how it has engaged me. As with most writers, I write from what I know and rely on personal experience and that of friends and family. They are the gifts of my life. Time to reflect on our life experience is the gift of what many are calling the third age. It presents us with the opportunity to examine, perhaps expand, and surely make peace with our interior lives.

I hope these stories, anecdotes, and insights will have a ring of truth, that readers will recognize their own experiences in mine, or that they will trigger relevant experiences. And that they will stimulate readers' own reflections about the gifts of their lives. Without prompting, people who have read drafts for me have responded with their own experiences, as have folks who attended my presentations. So there's hope for such a result.

In this regard, writing is a powerful means for reflection for readers to consider. As someone who has spent his adult life as a wordsmith, I favor having writing materials nearby and often find that when I record life's stories and anecdotes, surprising and unexpected details and insights emerge. I encourage readers to do the same and not to worry about style and form. Just write. Then rewrite to sharpen the experience and its meaning if you're so inclined.

To begin, what do I understand by the term *spirituality?* It's a common yet vague-enough term that embraces a wide variety of meanings, one that is even used to supplant religious affiliation as in the common refrain, "I'm not religious but I am spiritual"? You know that such a statement has gained much traction when Oprah Winfrey says it of her life and produces a series on spirituality for folks over fifty for her television network.

In its broadest understanding I believe spirituality deals with the dynamics of our hearts. We humans experience a puzzling imperative, an interior emptiness that we long to fill, one that has taunted humanity from our beginnings. Or at least since we began recording our stories and exploring what it means to be human.

Sixteen hundred years ago Augustine gave voice to this hunger in his timeless prayer "Our hearts are restless until they rest in You."

William James, American philosopher and very much a secular man, proposed in his book *The Varieties of Religious Experience* that tenets and practices are integral to religion. But he believed that the essence of religion was *psychological experiences*, and he looked for and proposed "states of consciousness" shared by all peoples.

More recently, Dean Hammer, a geneticist at the US National Institute for Health, proposes proof that religious behavior is innate and lays out a case in a book titled *The God Gene: How Faith Is Hardwired into Our Genes.*

It's a hunger recognized by all the major religions of the world. In the faiths of Abraham we find Mysticism in Christianity, the Kabbalah in Judaism, and Sufism in Islam. All are about the journey into the heart of God.

In the Christian context spirituality is about our ability to search for, sense, and respond to God's Spirit. It's about

- our relationship with God,
- our relationship with other humans, and
- our encounters with God's presence in our world.

It includes but goes beyond our Sabbath worship, beyond expressions of piety and devotion, beyond the sacraments that mark key transitions of our lives. I believe spirituality embraces our lives at all levels.

In my faith tradition, spirituality is most often associated with the monastic life and that of other religious orders. We have associated a spiritual person with someone who is holy, someone who separated from the world for a life of prayer, or someone engaged with the world in the advocacy of justice to improve lives through such services as education or health care. Only recently have we begun to decouple from the exclusivity of that view, to expand its learning to include the everyday experiences of family, work, play, charity, and intimacy. We have come to understand that through these we also encounter the signs of God's presence among us.

I write from a belief that prayer is much more than addressing volumes of words to God. It means being open to God's presence in everything we do. Or put another way, everything we do can be a prayer.

Jesus not only taught us to love God but that *God is love*. Think about the implications and power of that teaching. He also taught us that we must love our neighbor. Is there a connection? Can we meet God in our neighbor, in those we love such as a spouse or our children? Can this be a means to the union with God that we seek? Victor Hugo, the great French novelist, wrote "to love another is to see the face of God."

Charity, which is a concept for the commandment to love our neighbor, is at the essence of spirituality. Without charity spirituality can become one-dimensional, a kind of navel gazing. All the monotheistic faiths command good works. Judaism emphasizes justice for all, and the Old Testament teaches that justice precedes peace. The Old Testament prophet Micah tells us that all God asks of us is "to act justly, to love tenderly, and walk humbly with your God."

Islam, too, demands adherence to a strict code of care that is reflected in its names for God, such as the merciful, the compassionate, the generous, the forgiver. Charity is one of the five pillars of the Islam, and the term *zakat* refers to the duty to share one's wealth with the marginalized.

In Christian practice love of God and love of neighbor have spawned two thousand years' worth of good works, from the Acts of the Apostles to the local efforts to improve the lives of the marginalized to relief agencies such as the Salvation Army, Catholic Relief Services, and World Vision with worldwide reach. The great social movements of Western civilization such as the establishment of hospitals and orphanages, care and resources for the marginalized, schools, all grew out of this commandment.

How love of neighbor undergirds these efforts was demonstrated by Mother Teresa. When asked how she could continue her seemingly gruesome work with those dying on the streets of Calcutta, Mother Teresa responded, "The work we do is only our love for Jesus in action.

That action is our wholehearted and free service to the poorest of the poor, to Christ in the distressing disguise of the poor." In other words, Mother Teresa saw Jesus in the dying, rotting flesh of those she and her sisters picked up on the streets of Calcutta and cared for at Kalighat, an abandoned Hindu temple. Her practice of charity was a movement of human justice.

What do I mean by *spiritual exercise* or *spiritual practice,* terms that I use interchangeably?

The window, that everyday feature of our homes and workplaces, is a useful metaphor. We speak of the eyes being a window on the soul; Picasso's *Guernica* is a window on the horrors of war, specifically the Spanish civil war; in medieval times stained glass provided windows into the life of Jesus and the saints; and art instructors talk of portfolios as windows into a student's psyche.

Author Marjorie Thomason also seizes on this convenient metaphor to describe a spiritual exercise as a window—"a window on God's Grace." By this she means that age-old practices such as prayer, retreats, helping others in need, working toward an equitable society, offering hospitality, journal keeping, and pilgrimage are all "windows on God's Grace." They are means of revealing God's love, mercy, and favor. They are ways to help us connect with God.

So too with growing older. In the midst of this slow decline, I have come to see the possibilities of growing old as a spiritual exercise—another window on God's love, mercy, and favor.

While driving home from a visit to our daughter and her family in Florida, my wife and I stopped in Indianapolis to meet old friends for lunch. Despite the inevitable "organ recital" whereby we seniors chronicle and compare our ailments, catching up was delightful. Susan asked me if I was doing any writing, and I told her that I'd had some pieces published, one of which has led to invitations to speak.

"What do you talk about?"

"Aging as a spiritual practice."

"How do you approach it?"

"I look at five experiences of aging–diminishment, acceptance, intimacy, gratitude, and, and . . . and . . . " Uh oh, stall. I couldn't think of the fifth. Of course it came to me later. "Oh yeah, memory is the one I couldn't think of."

You get the drift. We laughed at this foible, so common among seniors.

So I will approach the subject through a prism that refracts memory, intimacy, gratitude, diminishment, and acceptance. Looking at them separately is a construct for the purposes of organization and, hopefully, clarity. In fact, they are all interrelated.

Two disclaimers:

First—these five experiences are not exclusive to this time of life. We can and likely do experience them at other times. However, in the evening of life's journey home I believe they take on different, if not deeper, hues due to time and perspective. I believe it is something we older people understand intuitively. The Pew Research Center recently reported that 61 percent of people in their fifties report that they pray regularly. After age seventy, 70 percent report that they pray every day. Given an expanded understanding of prayer as something more than a formula of words addressed to God, this number may be even larger. Perhaps it is this large because we are in a phase of life that we will not look back on as we do on childhood, adolescence, and adulthood. We do not grow out of this phase.

Nor are they the only experiences worth exploring at this time of life. They are, however, experiences that speak strongly to me

Second—I'm a third-age wanderer, a mediocre and sometimes dismal failure in most spiritual practices. In my writing I share my doubts with you and acknowledge—confess really—that when it comes to faith, doubt is usually my strongest certitude. Not that I am always in doubt. Occasionally my faith is like a laser—true, bright, and penetrating.

I don't often get it right. But at age seventy-five time does not stretch out endlessly in front of me. This makes me

- very aware of time left,
- time left to get it right,
- time that I've come to think of as vesper time.

When my then six-year-old granddaughter Shelby, awed by my age, told me in her sweet innocence, "You're so old, Grandpa," I recognized the truth as well as the blessing of it. Many blessings actually: overall good health, varied interests, a long-term marriage and a robust family, and engagement in numerous activities that challenge mind, body, and spirit. I'm here and grateful for this gift of time, or metaphorically, vesper time.

Vespers—or evening prayer—is the sixth of Christianity's prayerful celebrations of the day's progression and helps fulfill Paul's instruction to pray unceasingly. Vespers is observed at the time of the lighting of the lamps, just before darkness descends. How fitting! In this eighth decade the light indeed does fade, as do our capabilities and capacities. On the other hand, vespers is widely considered to be the most beautiful of all the prayers of the Liturgy of the Hours.

Vesper time is about continuing the quest. One of the seven major plots of Western literature is the quest. From Ulysses to Huck Finn, many of the great protagonists have answered a call to pursue a person, a value, riches, or perhaps a mythical place. On one level theirs are adventure stories portraying virtues such as endurance, courage, prudence, and kindness. We use synonyms such as *journey, search,* and *pilgrimage* to nuance such stories. On a deeper level these stories and their heroes are searching for meaning, for understanding who we are. Often the story is an allegory for an inward journey of self-discovery and spiritual growth.

Continuing the quest requires probing our memories for a call of one kind or another that we all receive. The call, I believe, is embedded in all human stories. It points to a universal journey in which accepting the call separates us from the familiar and the comfortable. It even separates us from the security offered by the authority figures of our early lives. It propels us into the unknown, where risks are taken, mentors sought, discernment practiced, distractions overcome, failures endured, successes celebrated, wisdom attained. It moves us into what becomes our life's narrative.

So, too, with this time of life, a time of grace and gratitude. We can still answer the echoing call. We can especially look inward. We can still reach outward. We can search for the spiritual essence that we may not have bothered with until now.

Opportunities for growth and learning are still very much a part of the landscape. I've been retired—if that's the right word—for over eleven years, and people often ask me what I do with my days. I use them leisurely. I'm not in much of a rush. I'm not busy and am often perplexed by those who say they are so busy in retirement that they don't know how they got it all done when they were working. Nor have I reached the stage where it seems that the less I have to do the longer it takes to do it. Well, perhaps that's so to some degree.

I live a life of privilege and try to be aware of all that it implies. I've been nurtured by a lifelong love; enriched by four beautiful children who grew up to be good people, leading good lives, doing good work; nourished by a rewarding career that included living in a culture and environment that expanded my worldview dramatically. It has all brought me to a life of leisured purpose. The lights may be dimming, but they are far from out. Health issues emerge now and then, and although they diminish me they won't likely finish me. I fill my days with reading, walking and/or backpacking, volunteering, traveling, writing, and seemingly endless home maintenance and yard work. For several years I continued involvement in my publishing career with occasional projects and board service, but that too drew down, as have my energy and my focus. When I have a few things to do and time frames to honor, I can get more easily frustrated than in my working years. I realize it's a good thing that I no longer have to deal with the demands of the workplace. Although I miss the relationships with fellow workers and authors I was fortunate to publish, I quickly put regimentation and the responsibility behind me.

I've come to understand something I once laughed at. While I was still working, I'd often call my retired sister, sixteen years my senior. I'd usually ask her "What's up, Sal? What's going on this week?" Her response ran something like, "Oh, I've got a busy week ahead of me." When asked how so, I'd hear about a doctor's appointment on Monday, shopping on Tuesday for a birthday present for (insert a name from a gaggle of nieces and nephews, grandnieces and grandnephews), lunch with Betty and Jean on Wednesday, an RCIA meeting on Thursday night, getting groceries on Friday. You get the picture. I'd chuckle at the fact that one daily event made a busy life for this very accomplished person who in her prime was a trail-blazing career woman.

Now that I'm retired I realize that such events give focus and shape to our daily activities rather than define them. Time simply takes on a different perspective. Eight hours doesn't seem like eight hours anymore. It seems less. Time is no longer the still water of our youth, a pool in which to play and soak. Instead, it's an accelerating river rushing to an indefinite destination. As I said—time left, time left to get it right.

1

Memory

*Life must be lived forward but can
only be understood backwards.*

—Soren Kierkegaard

esper time is my future arrived.

It's the present moment, a present moment
formed by my past.

As a spiritual practice, aging is about living into our
memories, about seeking their meaning, about accepting
and being kind to them. We do this through story, deter-
mining how our story shapes us, and by understanding
that we are more than the sum of our experiences.

Our story is not just a fact-based recall of events,
accomplishments, failures, growth, or diminishment.
It is also about recognizing an arc of nourishment, a
leading theme that fed the multiple phases of our past,
a storyline that fostered our growth and now helps us
understand who we are. Theologian Leonard Baillas tells

us, "The supreme achievement of the self is to find an insight that connects together the events, dreams, and relationships that make up our existence." Searching for that insight, that storyline, is an exercise is critical self-reflection. Like most spiritual practices, the discovery of what writer Thomas Merton calls the true self is a risky task. But without it we have no satisfying narrative. Without it we scuttle the chance to explain ourselves to ourselves, to discover what Merton describes as the person we can and should be emerging from the person we are.

At the same time, we need to acknowledge that memories are shape shifters. They are yesterday's snows. They fade, melt, and change their constitution, yet remain to be found in another form.

Vesper time is the time for such remembrance.

- Doesn't age allow us to see more clearly? We're no longer battered by the flotsam and jetsam of our journey in the world. Not that we've surpassed all problems. That's hardly the case as we deal with our diminishment. But we face less demand to "keep up" with a world that morphs and reshapes itself in continually compressed cycles of time.

- Remembrance is an entitlement of aging. In a very real sense we don't have to worry so much about where we're going, so we can and often do think about where we've been. Our experience has earned us a kind of healthy skepticism about our world and its ever-renewing problems and threats.

- We've divorced the world of work and even may have allowed ourselves to abandon the curse of busyness. We have more freedom and flexibility. We can find self-worth in something other than productivity once we put our hard-won identity of careers and relationships in perspective. A perspective that acknowledges that what we did, for better or for worse, was important then. But that was then. Life has become the present moment.

- It provides time to explore our own spirituality. The rush of life worked against this. Work and family, surviving or thriving in the present while preparing for the future, often leaves us feeling adrift, unable to think about our interior lives. With so many distractions now removed, we can pay attention to what life has told us, what our relationships with loved ones tell us, what our hearts tell us.

Exploring memory has a unique context for me and other members of my tribe. Sociologist Andrew Greeley once wrote that Catholics live in an "enchanted world." On one level Greeley referred to a "world of statues and holy water, stained glass and votive candles, saints and religious medals, rosary beads and holy pictures."

This was the world of my mom, a devout old-school Irish Catholic, who would rush through the house sprinkling it with holy water when thunder cracked and lightning flashed across the summer sky. Hers was a faith of Mass and devotions, prayers to St. Jude, and weekly trips across the Hudson to the shrine of St. Anthony ("that highway bandit," my dad would crack). It was a robed Infant of Prague placed on a hallway stand. It was spending Holy Thursday visiting the churches around the city with her, my younger sister in tow, to offer a prayer and a few coins at each flower-bedecked altar. This was the faith she imparted to her five children.

On another level Greeley believes that "enchantment" such as my mom's hints at a "deeper and more pervasive religious sensibility. . . . We find our houses and our world haunted by a sense that the objects, events, and persons of daily life are revelations of grace." In other words, God lurks in our stories. In remembering them we can uncover signs of God's love.

Church historian John Tracy Ellis calls this the Catholic imagination, a spiritual sensibility that is by no means exclusive to Catholics but is prevalent in the liturgical denominations, perhaps most richly expressed among the Orthodox churches. It's a worldview informed by the realization that God sent his Son to live among us. The legacy is a world, in the words of poet Gerard

Manley Hopkins, "charged with the grandeur of God." God embedded in the human condition.

This sensibility finds a rich historical strain in our culture—in the wonder of the startling Gothic cathedrals of medieval Europe; the laughter and tears of Chaucer's tales; the taking flight with Mozart's *Don Giovanni;* and the absorption with Caravaggio's painting *Rest on the Flight into Egypt.* In contemporary times we find this sensibility in the novels of Graham Green, Alice McDermott, John Hassler, and Ron Hansen; in the films of John Ford and Martin Scorsese. All is sacred. All is connected because all is infused with God.

Within such a realization, such a context, examining our own life story is in itself a spiritual experience. Our spiritual quest is to recognize this experience in the struggles between good and evil, in the elegance of our universe, in the beauty that surrounds us, and in our care and concern for fellow humans. In short, in the life we have lived and continue to live.

Our time-of-life questions are woven into the fabric of our past, especially our family and career—those major endeavors by which we attempted to leave something good behind. To examine our story is to embark on a journey inward, to review our growth in self-understanding, to embrace our failures and successes, to recognize our need for forgiveness and reconciliation.

And always to celebrate. For to celebrate, Henri Nouwen tells us, is to affirm that "underneath all the ups and downs of life there flows a solid current of joy."

However, exploring our memories requires a caution. It inevitably involves a kind of nostalgia that can be a dangerous longing, sentimental and cloying. Especially so when it presents us with a truncated if not skewed memory of a supposedly better world. Wallowing in a sea of ghosts misleads us.

And nostalgia can yield annoying results. We've all been subjected to the old codger retreading and retelling stories again and again, trying the patience of friends and loved ones who have heard them all too often. The German philosopher Romano Guardini warns us that the danger in which aging men and women find themselves is that of "living in their memories, of giving in to an existence which grows ever more empty." Yet despite these risks we have a penchant to engage in nostalgia once we are "of a certain age."

But what if we live out of our memories rather than in them? What if we explore what time has to tell us, not as navel gazing, but as a means of understanding what we have to offer? Can't nostalgia be a useful therapy when there are many more years behind than ahead? While avoiding the pitfalls of retelling old stories, can't nostalgia help us understand why we've become who we are, what happened after the forks in the road? The habits of the heart are formed through life experiences. Exploring memory confirms these habits, habits that foster the courage to face life's ending. During the time I gathered materials for this chapter and struggled with writing and rewriting, I had a vivid dream. In it I'm in my bedroom at the top of the stairs of my childhood home. I'm no longer a child, but my age isn't clear, maybe mid-teens.

Shadowy, indeterminate figures stand outside my door. When they get distracted, I run past them, down the stairs through the hallway, passing the fireplace and the old upright piano to the front door. Everything is as it was when I was a kid at home. I undo the safety chain, turn the dead bolt to the right, and open the door onto the enclosed small porch with a wooden storm door to the outside. But the storm door handle is gone, so I slip my finger into the hole where the handle should be and quickly pull the door open. The shadowy figures reach for me as I step out onto the snow-covered stoop, barefoot and in boxer shorts. I run down the snow-covered sidewalk toward the street. I see the glow of lights in a second-floor flat in an otherwise darkened neighborhood and run in that direction, toward the light. I'm yelling something when Sue wakes me.

I doubt that the shadowy figures were guards or that I was being restrained. They could just as easily have been figures watching over me as somehow protecting me. Parents, as I would learn, have a hard time lifting the protective curtain. But it's clear that the dream reflected my looking outward from a young age and my leaving home with few material resources to encounter and engage a world both strange and promising.

Childhood is the source of our sense of self. Reflecting on and developing our story helps us understand what it means to be human and perhaps determine if we have measured up to what God intended us to be. Mine was a once-upon-a-time childhood of discipline, responsibility, and conscientiousness. Which isn't to imply that it was grim or dark in any way. Laughter and good times permeate my recollections.

I was a bit of a counterpoint amid this family, a family that set great value on staying in place. My dad and both my brothers were in the military, had seen the country and been stationed in Europe and Asia, but all came home. They expected the same of me, another child who would grow from a taproot four generations long. I wanted to go away to college, but the finances were not conducive, so I became a "day hop" student at a nearby school. I hoped to study abroad for a year, but the family vision was not broad enough. I held jobs all through college, working full-time in my final year. As graduation approached I was offered a job in the local Associated Press wire service office, one that covered the state capital. But I was ready to leave, to plunge into a beckoning world, barefoot and in boxer briefs if necessary. Eyebrows were raised, tears were shed, and Irish guilt applied broadly. But I was inured. Within days of graduation my brother was driving me to New York, my father's encouragement and my mother's tears fading in the rearview mirror. From there I would cross the Atlantic by ship, barely twenty-two years old, a one-way ticket and four hundred dollars in my pocket.

I tagged along with a college mate who planned to finish his French requirement at a summer course in the Sorbonne. A student ship took us from New York to Le Havre, then a train to Paris, where I spent the first night in a park propped up against my brother's Marine Corps duffle bag. I had a touch of spunk, was short on French, and long on naivete.

Several wonderful locals—Gerard, Jacques, and Bernadette, surnames years beyond retrieval—befriended us and took us under their wings, found us an inexpensive hotel room, showed us the fresh market, and introduced us to the student dining facilities at the Sorbonne. For survival money I got a job selling the Paris edition of *The New York Times* in the afternoons on the Champs-Élysées or the evenings in front of a grand beaux arts structure that was then the Paris Opera House. I also corrected and typed letters in English for a small exporter and sold a series of articles on my experiences to my hometown paper. It paid the rent, provided money for espresso and beer, baguettes and camembert, and an occasional foray into Les Halles for onion soup and chilled white wine. I haunted the Louvre and the Rodin, practiced speaking my reader's French, hung out in a cafe or two on Boulevard Saint-Germain, and explored the city's parks, churches, and museums. Whatever was free. It became a six-week transformation, especially for an Irish Catholic kid from a circumscribed urban neighborhood. How my worldview shifted and expanded.

After a forty-eight-year hiatus I returned to Paris and spent several wonderful days retracing my youthful steps. I expected change and readily found it. It wasn't bad; it was just change. I wasn't chagrined by it. I walked the few blocks of Rue de l'Ancienne-Comédie, looking for the hotel where I shared a four-dollar-a-night room for six weeks, even asked in a small boutique hotel if it had once been called the Windsor. It hadn't. I think I entertained the fantasy that I'd encounter the always helpful African hotel manager who spoke French lyrically in a resonant baritone. He'd remember me and ask about my roomie. But the reality of the street quickly kicked in. The Windsor on Rue de l'Ancienne-Comédie is gone. The etched stone plaque remains, letting visitors know that the king's court jesters lived on this street through most of the eighteenth century. The old restaurant across the street is still there, looking much smarter than I recalled. But precious little else is familiar, a once sleepy side street buried in an explosion of tourist-related commerce.

The lovely Pont des Arts, an iron footbridge linking the Left Bank across the Seine to the Louvre, is shackled and scarred by thousands of padlocks, placed there by lovers, an over-weighted symbol of their fealty. Boulevards Saint-Michel and Saint-Germain are still wide and busy, minus the rickety Renaults and rusty Deux Chevaux of the early sixties. The side streets no longer provide quiet refuge. What a frenzy it has all become, the students who once sipped espressos in the cafes replaced by guide-toting tourists. Would Burroughs and Ginsberg find a suitable place to dally now? Would Sartre and de Beauvoir find a welcome table at Les Deux Magots? The Left Bank of Voltaire and Molière and Wilde is gone, replaced by gaggles of tourists treading in their footsteps.

The museums echo the frenzy. In that other time I stood within arm's length of the *Mona Lisa*, but now she was mobbed by a jostling semicircle throng fifty feet deep. They had no chance to sit in the presence of *La Gioconda* and seemed to be there to take photos to send the folks back home. An unobstructed view was hopeless, so I turned away from the dozens of phone cameras held high but offering little more than a periscope's view. I made my way to the quarter-mile-long Grand Gallery to linger nearly alone with works by Raphael and Caravaggio—masterpieces, not pop stars.

I took the changes in stride, I think, taking solace from the words to a once-popular song:

> Oh, the last time I saw Paris
> Her heart was warm and gay
> No matter how they change her
> I'll remember her, ah, that way.

After a stroll through a packed Notre Dame Cathedral, I sat at the tip of the Isle de La Cité and recalled young friends, names long forgotten; remembered our youthful discussions of politics, religion, philosophy, and music that wore long into the night. They challenged my sense of America. Our paranoia at domestic communism, our abysmal race relations, our consummate materialism were all easy targets of idealistic war-born European youth. Despite their challenges, these young people revered the United States and its promise, and appreciated the considerable sacrifice its people made for their well-being. They loved our movies and our jazz, the hope and vibrancy of the youthful Kennedy administration, Martin Luther King Jr.'s appeal to our better selves.

I think it was St. Augustine who wrote that the world is a book, and he who has not traveled has read only one page. In Paris I began to read the book that would shape my life.

On another day I decided to treat myself to lunch at the Café de Le Paix, where I once sold papers and couldn't even afford a coffee. I still couldn't. So I made my way to a more intimate sidewalk cafe, where I stalked the ghosts over white wine and onion soup gratinée—the kind with the bread on top covered with melted cheese that drapes down its sides. Memories surfaced despite my faulty recall of a more expansive Place de l'Opéra, of longer steps for an opera crowd in evening dress to ascend. In this same mind's eye I spotted the old woman beggar I came to know through repeated evenings of eye contact that led to smiles that led to waves. She'd wearily set herself to the ground at the Métro stop, hand held out in supplication for hours. One night she waved me over to ask how I'd done selling my papers. "Fine," I told her. Then, with a triumphant smile, she parted the pleats of her long, thick, black skirt to reveal buckets of change in her lap. Despite her revelation I opted to continue my career in print media, occasionally enjoying explaining that my first job out of college was with the Paris edition of *The New York Times,* always waiting a bit to explain that I had been a street vendor.

I recalled the American tourist who asked for directions and then complimented me on my facility with English. I thanked him and told him I'd been "educated in the States," smug in the belief I had passed for a local.

Then there was the IBMer who was incredulous at what I was doing. He gave me his card and wrote a name and number on the back. "Call my boss when you get back to the States. IBM is looking for people like you." I never followed up. I knew even in 1963 that gray flannel wouldn't suit me very well.

In my reminiscing that summer afternoon I was struck by how similar my family-raising, working-life years were to today's Paris—hectic, intense, purpose driven, squeezed full with people and activity.

And how similar my post-career years are to that carefree adventure in Paris so long ago. I realized my good fortune—that the evening of life has granted me a freedom unknown since youth. It's a bit like a second adolescence, this time around with the benefit of a more settled brain and decades of experience. Now I have freedom to pursue personal interests—to watch with pride the unfolding lives of our children; to enjoy spontaneous meetings with Sue for coffee or lunch; to revel in grandchildren's antics, observations, and conversations; to gain a richer understanding of music; to whittle down that list of books; and to travel. I can even plot and undertake occasional grand adventures, such as long-distance hikes and bicycle rides with old friends.

My memories have rekindled wonder, revelations of grace from an "enchanted world."

Such memories enforce my belief that my life has been charmed. How else can I explain stumbling into a rewarding career the way I did. In the late 1970s I held a job for which I wasn't a very good fit. And the "better fit" work I sought was scarce in northern Vermont, the place we dearly wanted to stay.

On Mother's Day (May 8, 1977) I called my mom to chat and wish her well. After a minute or two exchanging niceties, she asked, "What's wrong?"

"Nothing's wrong," I replied. After all, I was working and supporting our young family. Even though it wasn't an ideal job, I planned to eventually find something better suited to my skills and temperament. I had said nothing to her to indicate any level of dissatisfaction, and she didn't even have my palms handy to read!

The short version of the rest of her part of the conversation was to tell me she knew I was unhappy and that she was going "to start a novena today that you'll get a job at a good Catholic university." Only from an Irish mother! I didn't think much of it, other than to explain to my convert wife that a novena was daily prayer for nine days for a special intention. Then, on Monday May 16 (you do the count), I got a call late in the day from a former employer. Tom had just returned from a convention where he had dinner with an old friend and book publisher who told him he was looking for someone to direct his editorial department. "You're perfect for this job, Frankie," he said. "I told that to John Reedy. I told him that if I could afford to, I'd hire you and keep you on the back burner until I needed you. He wants you to get in touch." He gave me a phone number and added with unnerving certitude that the job was "mine to lose."

So I got in touch and flew from the mountains to the heart of the prairie for an interview at Ave Maria Press at Notre Dame. A good Catholic university even by my mom's rigid standards. The rest was my career until retirement in 2005.

Surely this too is Greeley's "enchanted world" revealing grace.

Time softens our memories. Many, especially the older ones, have a dreamlike quality. They're encased is a soft-focus haze with washed-out color, with a seemingly slow motion action. Perhaps it even distorts them. To demonstrate we need only talk with our spouse about our first date, or the day our firstborn came into the world, or any other significant event tinted in sepia. "I remember it well," you'll both say. But you'll both remember it differently.

Sue and I met at a youth hostel in the Monte Mario section of Rome. I was working there for bed and board, stranded without enough money to get home. She and a girlfriend were hitchhiking through Europe. It was a more innocent, safer time, soon to begin imploding around the assassination of a youthful president, the mire of a tragic tropical war, and the dreams and demands of a subjugated race seeking long-denied equality. She remembers meeting me as she registered at the hostel. I recall seeing her for the first time while serving dinner from behind the counter of the kitchen where I was working. She thinks she was wearing a blue top or a red dress. I say she stood there with Barb, all youthful ebullience wearing a lemon-yellow cardigan and light tan jeans. "That was one of the other girls you met," she quips. I thought we went to Pompeii together. She says she went with her girlfriend.

Now there's a level of charm to such discoloration of a memory that has little effect on the essence harbored within. What remains is the meeting and the journey launched. We did several things together in Rome, met again in Naples and visited Capri, Sorrento, and maybe Pompeii, and set off on a lifetime together.

In less than a year we married. I see now that almost every major decision, every significant life shift is rooted in the tenor and timber of those days in Italy, in who we were in that long ago autumn in the warm Italian sun. We found in each other a common sense of adventure, a willingness to take risks, little fear in being outside our comfort zones—whether finding passage home on Yugoslavian freighters, moving a young family to an island in the tropical Pacific for six years, encouraging our children to identify and pursue their own life paths. Perhaps the biggest risk was our decision to "settle down" into the stability of life and careers on a Midwest university campus.

When the inevitable rough marital cycles threatened, I'd find myself thinking, "Be patient. We're meant for each other. Don't mess up a love story like this one."

An enchanted world. A revelation of grace.

Not all memories are bright and endearing. Too many are dark and forbidding. Every year a Christmas letter from dear friends chronicles the lives of their children and grandchildren, including a line or two about an alienated child who has always rebuffed their outreach. But perhaps always will not be forever as our friends continually express the hope he will contact them one day soon.

We may carry a darkness in our hearts resulting from inadequate or dysfunctional parenting, abusive relationships, failed marriages, economic privation, or the scars of war. The source list is long.

Many Catholics carry especially painful memories rooted in blatant failures within our community: inadequate pastoral response to failed marriages or the shunning of those in new relationships that do not meet the norms of a rigid legalism; an institutional myopia toward woman and their full participation in the life of the church; the decades-long saga of clerical sexual abuse coupled with the leadership's moral failure to deal with it.

A very dear and long-time friend recently lost his middle-aged daughter to cancer. His son, who had been sexually abused by a cleric as a boy, stood outside the church for the funeral service, greeting people there. My friend says that the continued publicity around clerical abuse and government investigations has awakened his son's memories; he refuses to enter a Catholic church, even for his sister's funeral.

I dare not suggest how such memories are healed. It's beyond the pale of this effort. And there is a library's worth of books on the subject and a vast network of qualified counselors that offer appropriate help. But I do know that forgiveness and reconciliation are central to recovery. I've wondered what the perception of the sexual abuse scandal would have been if the hierarchy responded differently. Instead of spending vast sums on slick legal teams to stonewall the victims; if instead of impugning the victims credibility, what if it had gathered itself in a cathedral in one of our major cities, publicly acknowledged that grievous sins had not only been committed, but then compounded? What if the members of the hierarchy had collectively prostrated themselves on the sanctuary floor facing the congregation and begged the forgiveness of the laity and innocent priests that the hierarchy had betrayed?

Would exercising the church's own model of forgiveness—confession and reconciliation—have provided a more positive and hopeful context for healing?

Gandhi and King and Tutu and Mandela, towering moral leaders of the twentieth century, achieved wonders with their practice of reconciliation on a national scale. Imagine its potential within institutions and among individuals?

In a discussion after a presentation I did that dealt with dark memories, one woman spoke up to offer some simple advice: "Remember to concentrate the wonderful memories and bless them. Forgive the bad memories." Encouraging advice, but not easy advice. Thomas Merton reminds us that exploring the interior life is not a logical exercise. It means listening deeply and awaiting inspiration.

With a great deal of joy tinged with sadness I recall working with Lawrence Martin Jenco on the development of his book *Bound to Forgive*. Father Jenco was a priest working with Catholic Relief Services in Lebanon when he was kidnapped on the way to his office one January morning in 1985. Although it was a case of Shiite radicals kidnapping the wrong man, Father Jenco spent over nineteen months in captivity, enduring chilling deprivation and cruelty—beaten, often isolated, months chained to a kitchen radiator, six weeks in a clothes closet, blindfolded whenever captors were present, transported from prison to prison to prison wrapped like a mummy and slid into a spare tire compartment under a truck bed.

Yet within days of his release, when a journalist asked, "Father Jenco what are your feelings toward the terrorists who held you?" he says that he responded without much thought, "I'm a Christian. I must forgive them."

Shortly before his release one his guards asked him if he remembered his first six months? He says that Sayeed had brutalized him and that he responded, "I remember all the pain and suffering you caused me and my brothers." Sayeed had moved from calling him by his last name, to his first, then to "Abouna," meaning "dear father."

"Abouna," he asked, "do you forgive me?" Marty said yes, but also: "Sayeed, there were times when I hated you. I was filled with anger and a desire for revenge. But Jesus said on the mountaintop that I was not to hate you. I was to love you. Sayeed, I need to ask God's forgiveness and yours."

He described the scene—a blindfolded captive and a repentant guard sitting next to each other on a mat—as "two prodigal sons coming together" asking one another's forgiveness. One for brutality, the other for anger and thoughts of revenge.

Although he believed he had to forgive unconditionally, he also said that to forget was almost impossible. He wrote:

Jesus, the wounded healer asks us to forgive, but he does not ask us to forget. That would be amnesia. He does demand we heal our memories. I do not believe that forgetting is one of the signs of forgiveness. I forgive but I remember. I do not forget the pain, the loneliness, the ache, the terrible injustice. But I do not remember it to inflict guilt or some future retribution. Having forgiven, I am liberated. I need no longer be determined by my past.

Martin Jenco was a good priest and in many ways an ordinary man. When called by his principles, he rose to the extraordinary and forgave the bad memories.

And the arc that nourished me, my inspiration from remembrance?

I bless the concentration of so many positive strands woven into the fabric of my life. As I finger and sort them in my mind, I glimpse answers to the pressing questions of my time of life—who am I now? What have I become?

I'm Catholic born and raised, a product of my church's schools, a participant in the life of many parishes, and a worker in its fields. I'm awed by its riches, nourished by its mysteries, appalled by its vices, discouraged by its failures. I'm a man of faith, but a strained believer, holding sympathy with author Graham Greene, who observed that as he aged he had less and less belief

but more and more faith. I sense what he meant as time
and experience distance me from once-held certitudes.

My faith is a nomadic experience, far removed from
the certain, parochial religion of my youth. I grew up in
a northeastern city that was so Catholic that we identi-
fied by our parishes. Mine was an urban enclave of Irish,
Italians, and Jewish families. I don't remember becoming friends with a Protestant until I was in college. At
that, Ed was a Protestant attending a Catholic college. It
was a circumscribed world, existing almost as a parallel
universe to the secular one.

Although my faith is rooted in the faith of my youth,
I'm now less concerned about orthodoxy, more willing
to look for the metaphor in the literal, more willing to
accept the mystery of belief, more inclined to doubt.
Paradoxically, it is precisely because I believe that I
doubt. I find comfort in my doubt, knowing it enriches
my faith. After all, even Jesus's disciples were doubters.
I once thought doubt to be at odds with belief, a threat
to my certitude. I now see doubt at the heart of faith,
aspects of the same reality. Doubt doesn't mean I have
accepted Pascal's wager; I don't engage belief as a safety
measure. But the content of my belief races out then
circles back, grows and shrinks, shifts and twists around
an abiding presence from which I cannot stray. My daily
struggle, my daily quest, seeks understanding.

Certitude troubles me, while mystery enchants. I accept that some things are inexpressible and incomprehensible, a recognition of the inadequacy of language. That's why painters paint, sculptors sculpt, and composers compose. The nineteenth-century Austrian composer Anton Bruckner once wrote to a colleague, "I cannot find the words to thank you as I would wish. But if there were an organ here, I could tell you."

Strangely enough, my ignorance doesn't frustrate me. I take comfort from the sacramental imagination, or sensibility, that lies at the essence of my belief in Jesus. This is a worldview informed by the realization that God sent his Son to live among us. As Hopkins reminds us, God's grandeur will "flame out, like shining from shook foil."

This spiritual practice called growing older means listening to what our lives have to tell us, sifting out the chaff, watching for that quick glint of flame, and clinging to what has nurtured our growth. The reward? I believe that as we age—if we listen to life—our capacity for empathy increases. And that's the source of wisdom.

2

Intimacy

Your task is not to seek intimacy but merely to seek and find all the barriers within yourself that you have built against it.

—Rumi

"It's a chapter on intimacy. Start with something intimate," I told myself sitting at the kitchen counter doodling and hoping that something would come to me, something that would open up intimacy as a way to experience aging as a spiritual practice.

I need not look beyond the very setting.

It's a gray spring afternoon, overcast and foggy. The rain sometimes pounds, sometimes patters, but is steady for hours. And it's way colder than it should be. Time for a hot tea. Sue is engrossed in one of her one-thousand-piece jigsaw puzzles that always reside on a card table. Where she gets the patience for those things is beyond me.

"Tea?"

"No thanks. Not now." I can peel her an orange though, she suggests. So I do. It's one of those small pleasing rituals—a coffee in the morning, a glass of red wine at five in the evening, emptying the dishwasher anytime.

How ordinary yet how intimate.

Intermittent bits of mundane conversation puncture a timeless stretch: having leftovers for dinner tonight; calling our daughter in Florida to see how her father-in-law is recovering from an aneurism; getting together with friends on Saturday night for a local musical review; planning dinner tomorrow night for Lisa and Billy and their kids; emptying the dryer when I'm upstairs; making a phone call I really don't want to make. So banal, right? Then the not so mundane. Would I like apple crisp for dessert tonight? Silly question.

How ordinary yet how intimate.

Sue had a nasty fall this winter requiring back surgery and a prolonged recovery. She's a poster girl for joint replacements—five in nine years—and she's no wimp, always determined if not aggressive about her recovery. But this one hurt. She doesn't do lying in bed well, and she tried hard to tap her reserve of patience, for a while anyway. It annoys her that it's better if I help her with her socks, yet she thanks me often for being a good caregiver. I make light of it. "For what? I served you food your girlfriends and neighbors brought in."

How ordinary yet how intimate.

We took off for the day yesterday. Had lunch at a favorite spot, then went to a live butterfly exhibit in a huge glass arboretum. We forgot it was spring break, so there we were with seven thousand multicolored butterflies and eight thousand giggling, happy kids. Not sure which we enjoyed more. We found the butterflies enchanting, but grandparents really love other people's kids.

Passing a major mall without stopping is not a hill I'll die on, so we stopped "just for an hour." I found a chair amid other husbands and read a magazine, then wandered around a clothing store.

"Did you see something you like?"

"Yeah, a sport coat."

"Why didn't you buy it?"

"Too expensive."

She wanted to see it on me, so back we went to the store.

"It looks perfect on you. Why don't you buy it?"

"Because I'm seventy-four, retired, and don't have enough occasions to wear it."

Wrong answer.

The sales clerk seizes the opening and pipes in with something about a special 40 percent discount on Wednesdays. I'm not sure how he pulls it off, looking at me while talking to her, but I walk out with a new sport coat for my birthday.

How ordinary yet how intimate.

We know each other's drills. Fifty plus years together does that. Make no mistake—we still know how to get under each other's skins, which buttons to push to please or annoy, how to launch a barrage of low-level ground fire. We make the same mistakes. Over and over.

Ordinary intimacy is the practice of resurrection.

The thirteenth-century Muslim poet and Sufi mystic Rumi reminds us that being alive is "a state of rapture." Being here through these many years with a lifetime companion enhances the rapture. It speaks to the comfort of evolving from one kind of intimacy to another, from the heat of intermingled bodies to the warmth of intermingled spirits.

Ordinary intimacy with the one you've loved ever since you can remember is the first intimacy.

Somewhere through hard-won lessons of the passing years, we come to understand that there are no limits or conditions on love. Intimacy risks our emotional lives as we strive to free ourselves from ourselves for the well being of the other. Paradoxically, we gain strength through this vulnerability. We learn to pursue love, not happiness. Happiness takes care of itself. A Jewish proverb says that God didn't create us to be happy; rather, God made us to love. When two people love each other, when they expose themselves to the risks of love, doesn't happiness follow? Isn't love the goal, and happiness a result?

None of which comes easily. We are, after all, mostly self-centered and lazy practitioners. We know failure. Many failures.

Ordinary intimacy demands patience.

As far as we know, humans are the only species that searches for meaning. Without meaning our lives are empty, an emptiness sometimes addressed by repeated acquisition of things, a pursuit of satisfaction that only demands more acquisition. Yet the highly contrarian secret is that we find our richest meaning in loving, caring for, and doing for others. We are most fully alive when we open ourselves to others.

Ordinary intimacy is a source of meaning.

As believers we gather in mutual support for our journey to God. Here again we encounter the sacramental imagination, the worldview that has us celebrating what we sense but cannot fully grasp, the wonder of incarnation. God sends his Son to be one of us. Then Jesus promises that his Spirit will always be with us. Simply put, God among us. This is a spirituality that delights in our physical being rather than distancing us from it, and engages our world rather than isolating itself from it.

This worldview brings us together to bless life's major transitions, to mingle with our fellow believers, to discuss what's important to our community and what is not, to nourish one another's belief. It calls us to see to one another's welfare, to reach out to those on the margins, to fulfill the reign of God here and now.

We're social animals. We want to be connected. We want to love, we want to be worthy of love, and we want to be loved—in spite of ourselves. We're hardwired for intimacy, whose wonder and astonishment increase with age.

As much as we desire and pursue this ultimate expression of human relationships, so too, we believers desire and pursue an intimate relationship with God. We believe God knows us and loves us. But God is an impenetrable Silence, an indescribable Absence, an elusive Absolute. Such a situation begs the questions: Where do we look? How do we experience God? How do we fathom this known unknown who paradoxically knows and loves each one of us, Who calls each of us by name?

Mystics and poets through the centuries—such people as Hildegard of Bingen and John of the Cross—dedicated their lives to grasping this object of their consciousness, to the pursuit of personal union with God. They led lives of semi- to complete solitude—either in monastic settings or as hermits—centered on prayer and contemplation. Their writings reveal the need to abandon things of the world and to identify and abandon our illusions. Only then docs God enter our hearts completely.

They wrote of visions, of spiritual ecstasy, of illumination, of divine possession, of going where only love can go. Theirs are guidebooks— albeit inadequate—for the journey into the heart of God.

Contemporary mystics such as Thomas Merton, Simon Weil, and Evelyn Underhill pursue this same detachment and uncompromising commitment to love of God. Popular novels such as Ron Hansen's *Mariette and Ecstasy* and Ron Salzman's *Lying Awake* build on these themes and their attendant anxieties.

It's all very heady stuff, conveying a sense of other-worldliness centered on intimacy with the transcendent attribute of God—the realm of a fortunate few.

I cannot be counted among them. Such an encounter with the Divine is beyond imagining. Not in any sense have I been privy to religious ecstasy or radiant visions. As with most seekers, the wholly other God, a Being whose existence transcends our own, eludes me.

In our efforts to comprehend a God unlimited by time and space, we assign characteristics to God—father, mother, shepherd, midwife, potter, gardener, weaver— casting God in our image, or us in God's image. British writer G. K. Chesterton once said, "God made us in his own image and likeness, and we've been returning the favor ever since." Although useful, they are inadequate anthropomorphic labels. We are further frustrated in that our most dependable way of knowing has shown us how to split an atom, decipher a genetic code, and measure the expanse of the universe, but it has not provided a path to God. The rigorous analysis of observable data, the confirmation and reconfirmation of results, all required by the scientific method, yield no evidence.

On the other hand, science does not yet explain our sense of self, our understanding that we are embodied beings, that our soul or psyche is housed, so to speak, in a physical container—the phenomenon of thought and emotion that leads us to posit the existence of God. Meanwhile the idea of the location of the soul becomes a punch line or a tease at the expense of the searcher who grasps that despite all our scientific achievements we simply cannot satisfactorily explain ourselves by ourselves.

We may all be destined for ultimate and eternal union with God. The problem is now, a problem abetted by an orthodox tradition that defines God as love and emphasizes God as transcendent, unknowable, and beyond reach. Encounters seem to be realized only through altered states of consciousness achieved by the very few.

Yet our God hunger persists.

My hope lies in recognizing human intimacy as an opening to God. We can seek God's presence within the human condition, an attribute we call immanence. I take encouragement from an intuitive level of experience, whereby intimacy with another and with our physical world provides traces of God's immanence, where God's creation becomes a vessel of God's presence.

Immanence is a rich, if lesser known, vein in the Christian experience. Medieval German mystic Meister Eckhart taught that the Divine and Nature were inseparable. In his reflections we are, in fact, part of God. This comes from a man who was not a spiritual recluse, not a monk isolated within the walls in the exercise of life-long prayer, but a teacher and wandering preacher who wrote in his native language rather than Latin and told his students that intimacy with God was possible if you make the effort. It was so, he believed, because "God is with you everywhere, in the marketplace, as well as in church or in seclusion."

The twentieth-century spiritual writer and paleontologist Pierre Teilhard de Chardin echoes Eckhart when he reminds us that we are not humans in search of a spiritual experience, but rather we are spiritual beings "immersed in a human experience."

In Teilhard's and Eckhart's view, when the Divine and Nature are inseparable, we don't deduce God's existence; rather, we intuit God's presence. Creation is infused with the presence of God. Since the physical world carries the sacred within it, intimacy with nature and intimate human relations become windows on God's grace. We need to watch for them, recognize them, and embrace them.

Such intimacies are beyond fear. Fear that in a rational world we will seem foolish or even daft. We have to attack and dismantle those interior barriers we have constructed.

Rumi, who referred to his heart as a pen in the Beloved's fingers, captures the unitive nature of God and humankind:

> What a miracle, you and I,
> entwined in the same nest
> What a miracle, you and I,
> one love, one lover, one Fire
> In this world and the next,
> in an ecstasy without end.

John Muir is remembered as the Father of America's National Parks. Over his long activist life (he also founded the Sierra Club) Muir learned to read nature as he would a book, ever observant of detail and nuance. He believed that we need beauty as much as bread, "places to play in and pray in, where nature may heal and give strength to body and soul," while he fretted that modern civilization was destroying "nature, and poetry, and all that was spiritual." In the latter part of the nineteenth and early part of the twentieth centuries he actually feared "over-civilization." Were he dropped into the middle of today's world, he would likely say his fears were well founded if not fulfilled.

In the poetic expression of his mystical sense, he alluded to our oneness with the earth and the hand of God at work.

In viewing the Appalachian Mountains from the Cumberland Gap he exclaimed: "What perfection, what Divinity in their architecture. What simplicity and complexity of detail."

In proclaiming the beauty of Yosemite he wrote to his brother: "This glorious valley might well be called a church, for every lover of the great Creator who comes within the broad overwhelming influence of the place fails not to worship as he never did before."

Perhaps the poet Mary Oliver echoes Muir when she writes:

> I don't know exactly what a prayer is.
> I do know how to pay attention, how
>   to fall down
> into the grass, how to kneel down in
>   the grass,
> how to be idle and blessed, how to
>   stroll through the fields.

Finding a suitable place to engage with the natural world—Muir's "places to play in and pray in"—is not easy. Perhaps even wanting to find such places is more of a problem. It would necessitate weaning ourselves from our cars, curbing our addiction to screens, from hand held to wall covering, and detaching from the short-lived satisfaction of instant digitized communication and information.

Motivating ourselves to get off the couch and engaging in such detachment is not easy. I find walking a relatively simple solution. Just walking. Around my ex-urban neighborhood or into our nearby town. It requires little investment, just decent shoes and good socks, and an appealing place to walk that encourages intimacy with nature.

Walking in urban environments or suburban malls provides good physical exercise but does little for the psyche. For that we need to look to a continuum of areas that offer rich opportunities for nature's beauties and a large measure of solitude—city, county, and state parks; an ever-burgeoning network of bicycling and walking paths through the countryside; and our grand National Park and National Forest systems. We need to enter them, engage them, observe them.

We are not new to the healing powers of nature. For millennia we have sought places to go to be restored, to be made whole, from sacred pilgrimage sites such as Mount Kailas in the Himalayas to remote tuberculosis spas found from the Adirondacks to the Rockies when, not so long ago, TB was a widespread bane. Several of the Native American tribes in the Pacific Northwest traveled regularly to the area we now know as Glacier National Park to experience its healing powers. They even named the area Good Medicine. Today, movements are developing around such concepts as nature deficit and eco-healing.

The Japanese, one of the hardest working people in the developed world, inhabit a densely populated and industrialized landscape. But their mountainous terrain is covered with extensive forests where they have developed dozens of forest therapy trails. There they practice what they call *shinrin-yoku,* or forest bathing, as an antidote to their stress-inducing lives. They believe that green forests and blue waters relax them and offer them succor while actually abating physical ailments such as high blood pressure and mental fatigue. Research by their scientists is confirming such beliefs, enough so that Japanese corporations encourage employee retreats in the woods and by the water as means of regeneration.

Despite our careless and selfish efforts to the contrary, the beauty of creation still abounds and within it traces of God. After all, Yahweh says to Jeremiah, "Do I not fill heaven and earth?" (Jer 23:24)—not so much a question as a statement in the form of a question.

I'm particularly lucky to be blessed with a window on a world of beauty. It's literally a physical window that frames the elliptical moods of a vast inland sea: from the awe of its color-drenched sunsets to the menace of its black-clouded horizons; from its soft summer moon glades to its nearly trough-less foaming surf. It's a constant source of surprise, succor, and solace. Once it was a double rainbow in the western sky front lit by the early morning sun. I sat with it for so long that I was late for a meeting.

Another time it was a distant winter sunset viewed through the filter of falling snow in the foreground. As Sue and I watched it, noting it doesn't get any better than this, eight or nine deer strolled across the front yard nuzzling for acorns beneath the fresh snow. We recently had a full lunar eclipse. It's not often this coincides with clear skies in our part of the world, so there I sat in the pre-dawn October chill, jacket over robe, watching as the earth's shadow turned a nearly white moon copper high over Lake Michigan.

Sometimes when I gaze at the lake's moods on any given day, I feel as Merton must have when he wrote "I am drunk with the wilderness of the sixth day of Genesis," overwhelmed by God's work. The assertions of today's world mitigate against belief. Yet it's hard for me to accept that this detritus of the Big Bang is without cause. I warm to the poetic notion that we start as a stardust mite, as long as that's not all there is to it. An atheistic understanding strips us of any chance of meaning. It says we are accidents without purpose, the results of an evolutionary process without a cause.

I balk at such a thought. Must there not be some other intelligence, some great reality, what author Marilyn Robinson calls a "gracious intention," behind the evolution of a speck of stardust into a complex, albeit imperfect, human? How do we explain love? How is it that we're so capable of deep attachment to another? What is the source of goodness? Must there not be a deeper origin, an animating essence in all that lives? I'm drawn to author Mary Craig's belief in a "unity which underlies all created things and in a reality which is deeper than anything we can not know. . . . I believe this reality is the fountainhead of all that is valuable and good in our experiences."

I hope so. I want there to be. And this is my ever-present quandary, the fuel of my doubt, the fuel of my belief.

The modern world abuses belief in God. Wars are waged and heads severed in God's name. Some believe God died amid the carnage of the twentieth century. Its wars and ethnic cleansings made the Divine suspect. As we atomize and digitize our world, we seem to become its master, rendering God irrelevant. Religions, which are supposed to preserve and serve God's word and guide us into God's mystery, fail in their most basic charges. Religious institutions too often cultivate distrust rather than adherents. Meaning and mindfulness take precedence over spirituality and prayer.

I struggle with how God is present in the trillions of solar systems. Does such expansiveness, such timelessness, argue against God's existence? Is the Divine ours alone, or do other life cultures in the universe have their own salvation story? Must I suspend reason to believe? The answer of course is yes. How else explain the beauty of existence much less the existence of beauty? Matthew Arnold, a nineteenth-century British poet and social critic, in commenting on the mystery that is God notes that the word is not a "term of science or exact knowledge, but a term of poetry and eloquence."

Yet isn't our world without God a lonely world? Think of the isolation of Jesus as he faced his death and expressed his fear of abandonment, a moment of doubt in his own father.

It's a darkness that's hard to navigate.

But we persist.

At my level of spiritual growth I have no visions, but I recognize a vision. The *Pilgrim at Tinker Creek,* Annie Dillard, tells us that the pearl may not be sought, but it might be found.

I look up to see the buck standing in the drainage swale by the side of the road. He wasn't there in that same line of sight a few moments ago. I slow down, a slight chill of fear snakes up my back. He's huge. Where

did he come from? Why didn't I see him a few seconds
prior when I last bobbed my head? He stares, dark eyes
frozen on me, muscle and sinew motionless, large rack
pointing skyward. I'm too startled to count the points.
His size, his beauty, the shear surprise of unexpected
presence, awe me. But he drops his head and nuzzles the
ground for acorns, brushing away the snow, grandly indif-
ferent to my approach. Then he smoothly, slowly, sound-
lessly moves into the woods, camouflaged to invisibility in
the few steps it takes me reach where he had stood.

Rationally I can explain the deer. They're plentiful in
the woods and back roads where I live and walk daily.
Get real, I tell myself. There's nothing to it. But then
Merton tells us: "We have found places where the Lord
of songs visits his beloved. Crossroads. Hilltops. Market-
places." Could it be? Might it have been?

Such an encounter will spin my mind into wondering.
Wondering what he and I are doing here anyway? Wondering why any of us are anywhere. Is all this incredible
variety of life really just some accident of evolution, a
presence with no meaning? Or is it the result of some
intricate plan? I wasn't looking for a deer, yet I found
it. Is this one of Dillard's pearls? Isn't such a moment a
moment of prayer? Isn't such a moment a window on
God's love?

Intimacy with nature took on a deeper dimension
for me in my post-career years, a dimension discovered

while walking the Camino de Santiago with three long-time friends. We were "older guys," all in our mid-sixties, hailing from Michigan, Indiana, Alaska, and Australia. Graying and/or balding—although relatively fit—we saw the Camino as a challenging undertaking, a good gig with which to celebrate fortunate lives as well as actual or impending retirement.

So it came about one spring that I compressed sixteen pounds of my world into a backpack and, with these friends of thirty or more years, became a pilgrim. We set out to walk this ancient pilgrimage route that winds its way from the Pyrenees to the city of Santiago de Compostela, a major Christian pilgrimage destination. There, legend holds, the Apostle James the Greater is buried. Starting in the mountain village of Roncesvalles, close to the French border, we walked westward for five hundred miles. We had no guides, no porters, no support vehicles, not even reservations in hostels at our daily destinations. We allowed ourselves about thirty-five days and simply set out one Friday in April following way markers, ceramic tiles of all sizes and shapes with bright yellow arrows set in a royal blue field.

In the spirit of a pilgrimage I tried to make my Camino a walking retreat but wasn't sure how walking as a spiritual practice would unfold for me. How could a piously impaired man undertake such an endeavor?

Attend Mass or say the Rosary daily, or read the Liturgy of the Hours? Probably not practical. But then I don't think spirituality is confined to a life lived in relative silence in a mountain monastery; nor is prayer only the recitation of set formulas or participation in public worship. Rather, prayer and spirituality are lived daily in our work, our play, our deeds, our relationships—with God, with loved ones, with friends.

My spiritual exercise became simply to work at walking the best I possibly could, hoping that the discipline of physical exertion would enable spiritual results. My contemplation involved walking well for someone specific every day   focusing on my relationship with a loved one, a friend, someone who influenced or shaped me. The long quiet stretches gave me a chance to reflect on how each has enriched my life while I also examined the kind of husband, father, son, friend, or colleague I've been.

The result was a long, linear prayer, a process revealing my life's pleasant successes as well as its disquieting failures. It also provided an enriched appreciation of these same loved ones, friends, and acquaintances. It was all set against the backdrop of snow-capped mountains, expansive vineyards, endless fields of new oats, wheat, barley, and rapeseed; medieval villages marked by ancient stonework; steep climbs through mountain passes; such modern cities as Pamplona, Burgos, and Leon; and sweeping vistas of poppies, heather, gorse, lavender, and broom.

I cherished the long walking silences. They enabled a kind of detached view of self. I liked what I saw of my physical self—a sixty-something walking well, fit, quickly trail hardened, and successfully negotiating the unknown and unfamiliar. The view of my interior self was not as pleasant. Loneliness took a toll as I experienced my longest separation from Sue. I learned that I needed to evaluate habits of the mind, to develop my healthy thoughts and discard the toxic. A pilgrimage is, after all, a journey of self-discovery, an attempt to recover the true self from beneath our constructs of layers and masks. What is discovered must then be acted upon. The journey doesn't end at the pilgrims' Mass in the Saint James Cathedral or with a certificate of completion. As the poet R. S. Thomas reminds us:

> The point of traveling is not
> To arrive but to return home
> Laden with pollen you shall
> work up
> Into honey the mind feeds on.

My walking was neither an act of devotion nor an act of piety, but it was every bit a spiritual experience.

During the walk I stopped periodically to look back and get a different perspective on where I had come from. Now it's all about the perspective from looking back. The journey worked on me and in me, challenging my status quo. If I could manage for five weeks on the trail with sixteen pounds of stuff—including a pack and a sleeping bag—how much stuff do I really need to lead a balanced life? How can I adapt the discipline of the Camino, the excitement of waking every morning with a new destination over unknown terrain? They were days of possibility, and I try to apply that insight, to not ask myself what needs to be done on any given day but rather to ask, "What are its possibilities?" I realize that walking the Camino was a microcosm for life itself. I did well on some counts, not so well on others. Lifetime habits do not succumb easily to change.

I learned much through this personal seminal event and took many blessings into my future. I had prepared rigorously to walk the Camino with no expectation of continuing to walk when I finished. To my surprise I enjoyed it. I drew energy from fatigue, found stimulation in its routine, and took satisfaction in the accomplishment. And I learned that I genuinely like to walk and have been walking three to five miles daily for years. In that effort I find the lovely reflective time I could rarely find in the hustle of family living and career building.

Walking offers me a deeper perspective. It sharpens my awareness, yielding a more intimate sense of my surroundings. Instead of sweeping past the world at sixty-five miles an hour, walking offers leisurely movement—close up, intense, detailed—encouraging careful observation in order to savor the small, ever-changing joys of nature.

Most often the discovery is subtle; for example, north-country winters are not monochromatic. Occasional evergreens break through the whiteness, as do the red, orange, and yellow of hardwood branches and stems. Red and blue berries hang tough through the snow and the deep freeze. Rabbit, deer, and an occasional fox leave shadowy tracks in fresh snow. The impact of a clear blue sky's sun reflecting off the snow is stunning when our region's perma-cloud breaks up. The rotating seasons transform the swamp waters from murky to duckweed-encrusted green to dull, icy gray to a brilliant fluffy white sheet. It alone can seem a palette hinting at the presence of the master Artist.

As intimate as the experience of God in nature is, looking for God in relationships is most promising. The Psalmist sings a lament I expect we all experience:

> You hid your face;
> I was dismayed. (Ps 30:7)

How familiar. Don't we all experience God's absence? And I surmise we experience this absence more often than we experience God's presence.

Perhaps it doesn't have to be this way. Perhaps in our search for God we reach beyond when we ought to be just looking around, looking at our surroundings, looking at our neighbors, looking at our loved ones. Remember Hugo's insight "to love another is to see the face of God"? In engaging others we find the opportunities to emerge from ourselves, to choose selflessness over selfishness, to catch a glimpse of the face of God.

Henri Nouwen was a rare breed—a respected academic without a doctoral degree who had taught at universities such as Notre Dame, Yale, and Harvard. Rather than producing academic tracts he wrote insightful and popular books on spirituality. He died over twenty years ago, but dozens of his books remain in print. I visited him while he was teaching at Harvard Divinity School. Among the things we chatted about was a talk we had both heard Jean Vanier give that week at a conference in Boston. Nouwen knew Vanier, founder of the international L'Arche communities. Established worldwide, these communities welcome people with intellectual and developmental disabilities to live with people without such disabilities. They live "heart to heart," Vanier would say, not as provider and client.

When it was time to go, we walked downstairs to the exit. I had sensed that something was not quite right, and as we stood at the door I asked him if he was okay. His response took me aback. "My soul hurts," he said. He explained that while there was much talk and speculation about God at the school, there was very little effort to encounter God, to be with God. The work of the mind was ascendant while the work of the heart neglected.

This was not spoken as an indictment of the academy. Rather, Nouwen was coming to realize how out of place he was there. I didn't see it at the time, but he was saying that his academic career was coming to an end. I knew Nouwen as a kind, generous, and deeply empathetic man who could also be toughminded, especially when it came to negotiating a book deal. He had a touch of the mystic and was a world-class wanderer in his search for God. Within several months he would resign to take up residence at the L'Arche Daybreak Community in suburban Toronto. There he wove his own wounded life into the lives of the handicapped. Several years later I spent a long weekend at Daybreak with an energized Nouwen, a man much more at peace living "heart to heart" with his fellow community members. In the special human relationships nurtured at Daybreak, I believe Nouwen had seen the face of God.

As a spiritual exercise, for me this level of intimacy revolves around the question "Are you holding me, Lord?" By that I mean holding in the sense of cradling and its attendant notions of nurture, touching, and support. This may be my most fulfilling experience of God's love, if only because the answer is so often yes. A firm, blessed yes rooted in relationships that give me life.

I've been a husband for over fifty years, a father for almost as long. I suspect our four children know that Sue and Frank are counterpoint to each other. Our differences occasionally make us crazy, but we've grown and thrived through them, a long-term testament to the hook-and-eye model of marriage.

Where I'm somewhat reserved, she's gregarious; where I start a story at the beginning, she launches firmly into the middle. We both love people, yet social functions drain me while energizing her. I read mostly nonfiction, but she prefers fiction. And so it goes.

Yet we've united in a single purpose—marriage and family, extended and expanding, cemented by the belief, so insightfully expressed by author Valerie Schultz, "that the intimacy of marriage is the closest thing we earthbound humans can come to understanding the intimate way in which God knows us."

Schultz is in august company. Rumi continually attests that human love mirrors union with the Divine. In a lovely feat of double-entendre he prays:

> Last night I heard your heavy sighs
> It is within my power to end your
>   waiting
> to show you the way and grant you
>   access.

And Dante believed that two people loving each other is realized in the mutual love between God and God's creation.

Benjamin Franklin wrote to a young friend once that marriage is the natural state for humans. "It is the man and woman united that makes the complete human being." After describing the complementarities of male and female characteristics, he concluded that a single person "resembles the odd half of a pair of scissors."

Marriage is an evolving institution. Once its purpose was only procreation, both a biological imperative and economic necessity. This understanding worked well when life spans were short and children were needed to work the fields, shops, or trades, or to help provide family security. That model may still be necessary is some cultures. But even tradition-bound cultures have come to understand the inadequacy of such a sole purpose and recognize the necessity of mutual spousal support, both physical and emotional.

Yet even that is becoming truncated. Lived reality now shows a model that emphasizes the growth of the relationship and partner well-being. A family counselor and therapist once told me that she had concluded that the loss of respect was the most common contemporary deal breaker—not infidelity, not money, not emotional stress from the loss of loved ones, not addictions, although they all caused marital breakups.

In the pursuit and practice of intimacy, this evolving model recognizes the need for generativity and justice. It involves a relationship that is mutually respectful, mutually enriching, and mutually enhancing. Intimacy requires that we present our vulnerability to those we trust and that we do so fearlessly.

This is not an especially new insight. The correspondence between John and Abigail Adams witnesses a wonderful example of a generative relationship. Theirs was one of the great love stories of all time, aligned with Abelard and Heloise, Tristan and Isolde, or in truth wrapped in myth such as Lancelot and Guinevere. Through more than one hundred letters, they not only reveal their devoted love but demonstrate they were a team committed to mutual love, support, and equality while focusing on the goals of creating a home, raising a family, and running a farmstead. All while building a new nation.

So what about this holding, this cradling? Where is it nurtured? Closer, and more commonly than we may realize.

Are you holding me, Lord? Yes, when I get an unexpected call from one of our forty-somethings, sometimes with a question about a home repair or a problem or work; sometimes to tell us a grandkid anecdote or just to say "hi." Or as my oldest says, "Good rappin' with you, Pop." Or when the Laotian refugee who became part of our family calls Sue and me "Mom and Dad" or drops by unexpectedly when his business brings him near.

Are you holding me, Lord? Yes, when some idle mid-morning conversations in the coffee shop lead to the gathering of older men who want to explore the meaning of spirituality at this time of our lives.

Are you holding me, Lord? Yes when I sat with my comatose mom a month or so before she died. She had been in residential hospice care for several months and slipped into a coma. I took the overnight train to see her, and with my sister visited her that morning, hung around the family home for several hours, and then returned to the hospice later in the day to spend time before catching the late night train back home. My sister had spent many hours with her and talked to her conversationally, believing that we really don't know if someone in a coma has any degree of consciousness.

Sally slipped out of the room as it came time for me to say goodbye. I appreciated the chance to be alone with my mom, knowing this could well be our last time together. I leaned against the side of the bed, one cheek balanced on the mattress, a foot on the floor, my hand on top of hers. I told her who I was and talked to her, about what I don't remember. Then I told her I loved her, and to my surprise I could see a flutter under her left eye lid.

"Don't struggle," I said to her. "I know you know who I am."

A tear emerged from the corner of her eye, slowly trickling down the crease of her nose and cheek. It was the last time we were with one another.

Are you holding me, Lord? Yes, when a grandkid tells me, "You're so excited to see me"; or when another sits on my lap, head on shoulder, watching Sponge Bob with me; when the kindergartner, who laughs so easily at my goofing around, tells me I'm on her "silly team," the prestige of which is made clear when she tells me who else is on her silly team. I felt like a pitcher who has thrown a shutout in his forties—I still have it! Or when a nine-year-old grandchild sitting next to me at a restaurant table tugs my sleeve for attention and says, "I love you, Grandpa." "I love you too, Dan."

Are you holding me, Lord? Yes, while walking the Camino de Santiago, specifically while making our way through the expansive hills of La Rioja. It had rained heavily the previous day, and we had slogged through red mud for hours. The new day had started with more of the same, but around midmorning, as we tracked up a long, open trail, the clouds gave way to spreading patches of blue. A breeze picked up at our backs. We could see the red-dirt Camino, spotted with walkers, unfolding miles ahead over the broad, rolling hills. It cut through multi-shaded fields of green—early wheat, oats, or barley—occasionally interspersed by bright yellow rapeseed plots.

I realized I was walking the Irish Blessing— the wind was at my back, all things were green for me, the road rose up to meet me, and God held me in the palm of his hand.

Are you holding me, Lord? Yes, on a rainy, chilly spring afternoon when I grasp just how ordinary intimacy can be and appreciate that its low-key pervasiveness binds two long-time friends and lovers.

I wonder if, as we age, intimacy doesn't become more recognizable? Aren't we more adept at assessing the risks and rewards of intimacy? Isn't the appeal of grandchildren that they offer us an unconditional intimacy? Haven't the years made us more facile in reading character and personality traits? Don't we recognize more quickly someone we went to different schools together with? Or recognize more quickly someone whose different world will expand ours? Or, conversely, that there is little to interest and attract one another?

Growing in intimacy involves risk, and we age badly when we stop taking risks, when we do not engage new experiences and make new discoveries, when we fail to draw down our own treasury of knowledge and skills. This means being vulnerable in the sense that vulnerability leads to growth. Especially growth in relation to old friends and new ones, to those we love. These too are our openings to God. It means acknowledging that we have not yet become the person God intended us to be, that we will be a work in progress until the last breath.

I don't claim to get any of this spot on. Perhaps not even close. My doubts soar when I acknowledge my use of soft language in exploring a non-mechanistic and non-measurable world, a world where love is the only real thing. But I do get glimmers. Glimmers of hope. That there is a God. That this God is a part of our world. That in some mysterious way this God loves me. I struggle for words, for concepts that freshen my imagination as I escape childhood-induced notions of God.

In this evening of life's journey home, amid the madness of kings and the demise of institutional competence, in the era of repudiation of nearly everything, my faith is captured in Hopkins's words that "the Holy Ghost over the bent World broods with warm breast and with ah! bright wings." My hope lies in Jesus' promise to be with us always, that we are one with him, that he is in our DNA, that he sustains us in the Eucharist. What could be more spiritually intimate than receiving Christ in the Eucharist? That's why we call it communion, a sharing in common. In an empirical age such sustenance lies beyond reason, nestled in the lap of mystery.

3

Diminishment

But the best imaginers are the old and wounded,
who swim through ever narrowing choices.

—Freya Manfred

y friend Lenore is a very accomplished woman. She's smart, articulate, and attractive, a university professor whose accomplishments earn her research grants and invitations to conferences around the world. Now in her mid-seventies she continues her career at a campus far enough from home that she stays there several nights during the week. Yet she manages to return home on Thursdays and orchestrate the weekly Sabbath dinners for her family—a nuclear family of about a dozen people who gather every Friday evening.

While dining in a restaurant not so long ago, she was struck by the attention the waiter paid to her forty-something daughter. "It's like I wasn't even there," she remarked wistfully, no doubt remembering when that was not the case and noting how common such incidents have become. Like most of us seniors, she is becoming invisible.

Most of us experience it to some degree. Years of work, accomplishments, and experiences fade . . . then fade some more.

The loss of physical attractiveness and capacity is a slow atrophy for most. We can resist it, slow it down, fight it, but we cannot stop the retreat, even if we could pay the price of Dorian Gray.

The process of becoming invisible is benign diminishment, a mere glimpse of what might yet be coming. But as a noticeable step in our decline, it can be disconcerting.

Ask any of the half-dozen older men you might see mornings in the local diner. Their identity is no longer shaped by jobs and careers or by growing children who long ago left the nest. Their conversations circle in and out of politics, kids and grandkids, health issues, sports, the weather, and travel. Few outside their circle seek their counsel. A television talk show may set up shop in their cafe some morning, attracted by an election or nearby sporting event, but they aren't invited to the mike. They know they're becoming invisible. Except for perhaps the waitress, who fends off their wisecracks, ribs them, and keeps the coffee coming.

Ask any one of the five of us in our small men's group. All of us had rewarding careers—two physicians, a chemical engineer, a small business owner, and a book publisher. But it's past tense. Our businesses and professions moved on as we stepped off the train. The memory of whatever success we had, whatever good we did, whatever mistakes we made, is dimmed, both for us and for the co-workers with whom we once shared coffee or discussed projects and problems at one another's desks, in the hallways, or at staff meetings.

Michigan now has a law requiring everyone, no matter his or her age, to show identification to purchase alcohol. I don't get asked, even at the self-checkout when the six pack sets off the annoying electronic beep calling for an attendant. She just walks over and overrides the register without even acknowledging me.

Or when I am noticed, it's not the way I expect or want. I'm surprised at how often I've boarded public transportation in recent years and had younger people offer me their seats. Now, I'm delighted that such courtesy is still alive and well. But then so am I. People just make assumptions about us older folks—some good, some not so good. I know. I did the same thing. Ironically, one recent seat offer came a few days after I completed a sixteen-day backpacking trip that included numerous days in fairly strenuous terrain. I politely declined. I also declined the impulse to tell her that I'd just walked 235 miles carrying a full backpack and could ride like any other strap-hanger.

The Japanese military apparently has an interesting retirement ritual. At the ceremony for a retiring officer a fellow officer faces him and thanks him for his years of service and his accomplishments. He then grabs the retiring officer by the lapels, shakes him, and tells him in effect, this is now over for you. "Your work here is finished." Go and become part of another community.

You have to admire the power and honesty of such a sendoff and think of the movie *About Schmidt*. Remember Warren Schmidt? He retires from his career as an actuary at a low-key thank-you dinner and an invitation to "come back and visit us." When in utter emptiness he returns to the office to answer any questions his successor may have about the job, the new man is perplexed, giving him a look that says, "Did you really think we expected you to return?" The new man has no questions and doesn't know what to do with him. Poor Schmidt no longer belongs, but he hadn't a clue. There was no adequate closure on his career. Of course, this is only the tip of iceberg for this Thoreau prototype who lived a life of "quiet desperation" and then struggled for companionship and relevance in retirement.

Schmidt portrays another kind of diminishment, a diminishment of purpose. Gone is the regimentation and responsibility of the workplace. Most of us are glad to put those aspects of work behind us. But also gone is the purpose that was rooted in mission and commitment. And without purpose we drift into malaise. To counter this we have to foster new growth through volunteer work and service activities, travel, hobbies, and reading. Even the pursuit of spiritual growth. Within the realities of our compressed capabilities, interests, and desires as we get older, it's possible to expand our interior lives.

When I retired from publishing I immediately missed the relationships of the workplace—fellow employees, some of whom I had worked with more than twenty-five years. I also missed the wide range of authors with whom I was privileged to work. There is nothing quite like watching and/or helping a writer develop an idea into a book and then presenting it to the world knowing that it would enrich or improve lives.

As with Schmidt it's easy to be cast adrift, to not see ourselves in the same light as part of our identity is lost. Retirement sendoffs are a culmination of good will, the opportunity for workers and owners to say thank you and wish you well. They can easily leave the retiree with a feeling of "wow. If I knew they felt this way about me, I wouldn't have retired."

I waited seven months before I took up the invitation to "come back and see us." It was a lovely return, with former workmates being gracious and warm. But differences were playing out already, changes that could make for better operations and an altered environment. It was the opportunity to shake my own lapels and understand that this was over for me. I knew that in my mind when I walked out the door seven months prior. Now I knew it in my heart.

It seems clear that as the door to job or career closes behind us, we must open another, a door that accommodates a shifting identity. This isn't a simple matter. It implies an element of risk at a time we are becoming more risk averse. It may also evoke engagement nearly as intense as the workplace. Might that not be self-defeating? After all, we don't want to miss the delightful opportunity to escape the tyranny of busyness and the plague of productivity. I was a manager for much of my career and was well aware of the need for personal and staff productivity and thorough, yet efficient, systems. It was all part of the dogfight to thrive and grow, something I was ready to leave behind. That's not an easy adjustment. When I asked a newly retired acquaintance how he was doing, he laughed and said, "It took me six months to understand I didn't need to be productive anymore, at least not in the same way."

Much is involved in preparing for life's final act. Society places understandable emphasis on financial security, planning adequately so that we have enough to be comfortable and not outlive our resources. And there's lots of available advice in this realm. Little advice, however, is available for the emotional preparation and for the spiritual preparation. Everyone's experience is unique, usually reflecting his or her physical, emotional, and economic conditions.

In part it's a matter of finding the balance between our need to be needed and the chance to pick more daisies, between the benefit of continuing to exercise long-honed skills and the serendipity of journeying inward to discover who we really are. What we'll likely find is that complete leisure will not be what it looked like from the heart of our work world. Nor will doubling our screen time, as happens with so many retirees.

If we're in relatively good health many doors beckon: recreational or avocational doors to long-delayed interests. Doors labeled NEEDS to volunteer time and skills to help others improve their lives. Giving back is a constant theme with rewarding opportunities among those who have left jobs behind. And in an age of energetic, educated, and experienced retirees, this is a valuable resource for our communities.

We are blessed to be members of the longest-lived generation in human history. Many of us live within memory of life expectancies in the forties and fifties. Like all who have gone before us, we are in a phase of life we do not pass through. Unlike our passages through child-hood, adolescence, young adulthood, and middle age, we can now only pass on. This invites us to live in the present moment and acknowledge that we are as young as our dreams, not as old as our personal calendar.

Jean is a firmly established member of our aging cohort. On joining us one morning in the coffee shop she an-nounced that she was going to Philadelphia the next week with her grandson "to see Pope Francis." She had pursued tickets only to find out that there were none, that the event was open to any and all. Undeterred, she planned to take her petite five-foot frame into a free-for-all gathering of several hundred thousand in the hopes of catching a glimpse of Francis. She had even bought a couple of three-legged folding outdoor stools to rest on. We expressed admiration for her courage and resisted any suggestion that she might be naive.

I saw her a week or so after the visit and asked her how she had fared.

"Wonderful," she said.

"Did you touch the hem of his garment," I teased.

She smiled and said she would email me a photo. It was smashing. There she was, snug up against the man in white, both flashing broad smiles, two testaments to the young at heart.

On the other hand, our slow diminishment also offers us the opportunity to pursue what spiritual writers since the desert fathers have called the death of self. Since we are no longer players in the field, since who we are is not so tied up in what we did, since we are not so noticeable any more, why not engage in the spiritual quest of abandoning our egos? Who and what we are now becomes a spiritual question.

John Adams saw this. As an old man, long removed from nation building and governance based on the radical idea of human equality, he wrote:

> I find my imagination . . . roaming in the milky way, among the nebulae, those mighty orbs, and stupendous orbits of suns, planets, satellites, and comets, which compose the incomprehensible universe; and if I do not sink into nothing in my own estimation, I feel an irresistible impulse to fall on my knees, in adoration of the power that moves, the wisdom that directs, and the benevolence that sanctifies this wonderful whole.

Becoming invisible may be our first humiliation, but it's one that pales in the face of the physical diminishment and eventually the suffering that will likely accompany it.

I'm well into my seventies now, placing me into a time of both diminishment and opportunity. I used to be five foot eight but am now compressed toward five foot seven thanks to the inexorable pull of gravity and a fractured disk in my mid-fifties. Names, dates, and past events come more slowly as synapses misfire. And as my wife likes to tell me, I'm often in the "hereafter," as when I walk into a room, stand, look around, and ask, "What did I come here after?" Unless I leave stuff in a pile by the door, I often walk off without it. My car keys, glasses, watch, and cell phone have feet that take them to unlikely spots. Some technical genius recognized my condition and developed a car key fob that links to a cell phone. Get an app and the phone will find your keys. But what about my glasses?

Lists keep me on task more than ever if I remember to take the list with me on errands. Telltale slips of paper lie near the phone, in a pocket, by the computer, in the car door's pocket—call Humana, two fourteen-ounce cans of diced tomatoes, dinner with Bob and Liz on Friday? return Sally's call, reserve a room for the fourteenth. And on it goes.

An autoimmune condition layers fatigue over many of my days and imposes soreness on joints and scalp, all the while promising permanent companionship. I've had one cataract removed and another is primed and ready. Retinal surgery that developed a staph infection loomed like one of those highway warning signs: DAN-GER: Construction Ahead. In my case, Reconstruction Ahead. Parts will break down and need to be repaired or replaced to make my long road longer. Momentary lulls invade my speech as I unscramble my thoughts or search for the right word. My memory is a curious thing yielding the sequence of the 1988 national champion-ship season but unable to quickly bring up the games I attended last year.

My hair has thinned and shows only a remnant of pepper amid a preponderance of salt. I use the crummy-tasting toothpaste that desensitizes my teeth to heat and cold. I wake up too often during the night. I regret the wrinkles and sags brought on, in part, by the years in the tropical sun. Embarrassing hairs poke out of odd places on my head, and aging experts tell me I can expect my ears and nose to continue growing. Swell! It bothers me that the older me is what my kids and grandkids will remember, perhaps expressing surprise when seeing photos of the younger me. I vividly remember their reaction, when as twenty-somethings they saw a World War II photo of Sue's father in his navy uniform. "Wow, Grandpa was a good-looking dude," they exclaimed.

By the time we reach into our eighth decade, we all have an address book full of information slowly being rendered useless. Many friends have died, others have fallen off our radar as the years sped by. This loss of family and friends diminishes us. The known losses are often deeply saddening. The suspected losses are frustrating. Christmas cards and inquiries go unanswered for a number of years; emails are returned as undeliverable. We may never know what has happened to them.

Friends from our neighborhood moved to Austria many years ago, but we would see them every summer when they returned to visit family. We even spent a week visiting them in Vienna. As their kids spread out, they didn't have time to stop in Michigan. One year no Christmas card came; the next year ours was returned. I didn't know specifically where their daughters had settled, and I finally remembered a mutual acquaintance and called him. The worst had taken place. Jack had died, and Lisle was living in an Alzheimer's care unit out West. Our circle, which grew ever larger through our lives, now contracts.

How can diminishment inform my spiritual practice of aging? I find opportunity and perspective. Two insights offer hope:

Carl Jung tells us that "the greatest and most important problems of life are fundamentally unsolvable; they can never be solved only grown out of." As we grow out of them, we grow out of anxiety.

Merton reminds us that God waits for us in silence and that God waits for all of our inner noise to exhaust itself.

In these two insights I find a cause and effect. If Jung is right, then I've outgrown a lot of unsolvable problems. I've let go of them, such as issues that involve control, the pursuit of worldly success, or what Merton calls "the poisonous urge to change everything." I try, not always successfully, to offer advice to offspring only when asked, keeping in mind that although I'm not done loving them, I am finished raising them. Now, to Merton's point, that's a lot of inner noise that has exhausted itself.

Perhaps Merton and Jung were echoing the wonderful promise of Job: "Wisdom is found in the old, and discretion comes with great age" (12:12, NJB).

Does this mean I'm gaining on my ego? Perhaps. Spiritual writers since the desert fathers write of the death of the self, the need to transcend our self-interest in order to find union with God. Is this our opportunity? Why not abandon the ego? Why not let go of life's apparent illusions? It's no easy task. Illusions are real in that they captured my commitment and energy. The discretion comes in my attempts to sort through them, to jettison what's no longer important, to acknowledge with Jung that it's time to grow out of them.

Am I drawing closer to God in my paradoxical journey of discovery? I hope so. It does mean my time is available for different uses, and I can bring a life of experience to bear on such questions that surface with age.

And that's where our small discussion group fits in. We all retired willingly. We all miss aspects of our work life but knew it was time to leave that dimension of our lives. Serendipitously we found our way together through a sense of "Now what? What did I miss in the throes of career building and family raising that's discoverable now? What do I do with this gift of time?" Enriching meetings have found us ranging across discussions of religion, spirituality, spiritual practices, story, and grace.

I've quickly come to learn there are others who share my questions and perspective. I feel I am at least moving into what Merton calls *Kairos*—"the time of possibility and abundance"—and walking towards his precious Silence. Literally.

I mentioned that I walked the Camino de Santiago. It was on that thirty-five day, five-hundred mile trek that I became aware of walking as both a spiritual exercise and a new way of seeing. It has become my near-daily routine in the years since the Camino.

By spiritual exercise I don't mean an act of devotion or piety. Mystics and monks going back to Benedict teach us that the discipline of the physical life enables spiritual results. In walking I challenge my body and stretch my spirit.

Melville writes, "Silence is the consecration of the universe"; C. S. Lewis that "silent prayer is the best." In walking I find this silence while the act of walking becomes a silent prayer.

I start by simply walking the best I can. I set goals, usually related to time, distance, and physical carriage, while avoiding a sense of being on a forced march or a marathon. For an hour or more most days I get the chance to tame the chaos of my mind. To settle it. To focus. The contemplation in walking silences allows a detached view of both the physical and interior self. It provides the opportunity to jettison the negative—the annoyance of perceived slights, the frustration with societal ills, even the silly Walter Mitty daydreams.

Walking is a linear contemplation, a process that reveals my life's pleasant successes as well as its disquieting failures. It also provides an enriched appreciation of loved ones, friends, and acquaintances as I reflect on what they mean in my life. It offers another mode of my journey of self-discovery, an opportunity to glimpse the true self from beneath the constructs of layers and masks, a discovery that must then be acted on.

I realize that these diminishments I reflect on are quite benign. I don't want to give the impression that I'm naive about the ultimate diminishments that rob us irreparably of physical and/or mental capacities. I've watched in awe as the woman I love has fought back from breast cancer and become a poster child for joint replacements. She makes courage and tenacity look easy, perhaps too easy. Sue is the beneficiary of modern medicine. Without it we might have lost her years ago, or certainly would be now helping her about in a wheelchair.

As much as modern medicine may allow us to live longer, it also allows us to die slower, sometimes to horrible effect. And this is not just lived out in such cinematic events as the torturous movie *Amour,* a lesson of which is that we cannot engage the diminishments of age in isolation. It lives close to home. Both my mom and my dad suffered such indignities as amputations, strokes, and coma in their months of painful exit. My two older brothers both endured COPD and lung cancer. Sue's dad suffered the nasty slow goodbye of congestive heart failure. All their deaths were difficult, painful, and prolonged.

And the factoid generator tells us that if we live long enough, to eighty-five or longer, more than half us will suffer from dementia.

I am unsentimental about such inevitabilities, and I have no idea how I will experience spirituality and love of God in their throes. I know the interpretations of suffering, and know that our tradition portrays it as redemptive, an opportunity for growth. But aren't they easy promises when we have not had to care for a demented spouse, or are not experiencing the slow suffocation of congestive heart failure? I know I can't judge their efficacy. Not from my current vantage point.

Will my optimism about aging as a spiritual exercise evaporate in the face of real debilitating suffering? The bottom fell out for several very long hours when I realized I was in real danger of losing an eye to a staph infection. In short, will I have the courage I see in others?

In story after story of physical and mental diminishment I encounter courage, very visible examples of growing old as a spiritual exercise. Courage is, after all, a heart word, rooted in the Latin *cor* (heart). I see courage as the habits of our hearts overcoming the rationalizations of our minds. It's the heart's desire effecting what is good though the odds be daunting.

It's the choice to take the road less traveled.

It's what Chesterton meant when he described courage as "a strong desire to live taking the form of readiness to die."

I find hope and inspiration in the courage of others who at Vesper Time stand up to suffering and diminishment, accept its reality without crumbling into whiny self-pity.

Bill offered his story at a meeting in Chicago where I presented a talk on the spiritual practice of aging. A year before he had been unable to walk, the result of six years worth of stage four cancer complicated by degenerative arthritis of the neck, spine, and feet for most of his adult life. He was hospitalized and in rehab for a month. His primary care doctor told him he should look into hospice. Friends told him they didn't expect him to recover. But Bill had other ideas.

"Although I was in pretty bad shape, I expected to recover." He says he had two advantages: tremendous prayer support and a determination to resume a normal life as best he could. After rehab he progressed into a wheelchair, then to a walker, then a cane.

Soon he was working out at the health club even though he was still getting chemo treatments and hormone shots, bone infusions and blood transfusions. During this recovery he also had to be treated for a "botched knee replacement" and gastrointestinal disorders. I believe Bill had dark moments, moments of despair. He also had grit.

His oncologist uses Bill as an example to other patients and told Bill he expects that "you will be going to the health club three days after you die."

Although I remember Bill as pale and thin, he was clearly vital. He had gone back to a part-time job and was riding his bike again. At age seventy-seven!

His perspective through all this? It's rooted in a deep spiritual courage.

> I'm blessed and thankful to God. I'm closer to the Lord. I accept the limitations of age but I do not and will not define myself by my illnesses. I'm not a cancer victim or survivor. I'm a child of God and take that as my identity. I look to see what's ahead, not what's over.

I met Beverly less than a month after her sister died. Public transportation is lean in our area, and she needed a ride to the doctor's office. As with most first meetings, weather was a safe topic, especially on a bitter cold January day in an already epic winter. She mentioned offhand that weather had kept her and other family members from her sister's funeral in Chicago. The plumed snowmaker that hangs over the center of Lake Michigan had been dropping feet of snow on the counties of the lake's southern tip and turned the family back home. The sadness of her most recent loss was compounded by the death of her brother-in-law a few weeks before her sister, and the loss of that couple's daughter a few months earlier. And her mom had died the previous June. And these were only four of seven relatives who had died in the previous year. Tragedy pervaded her life.

But it was only the beginning of her story, which unfolded in subsequent trips to the doctor. She suffers from fibromyalgia, a disease marked by chronic, debilitating pain. And in her case the deterioration of her spinal column. She has had the condition for fifteen years and spent two of them bedridden. Disabled, she could no longer work.

A petite, late middle-aged woman, she gained a lot of weight and realized that "this had to stop." She forced herself out of bed and began her slow march back to engagement with the world. Her tenacity is daunting. She goes to a wellness center several times a week for an exercise regimen. Her pain is managed by morphine, so she has to have her blood tested monthly as a way to insure she's not selling her medications. She speaks positively of getting better, or at least well enough to volunteer at the local senior center. "So many people have helped me that I need to help others."

Despite facing the triple threat of medical disability, chronic pain, and economic hardship, this single mom has raised three children, two of whom have careers in health care while the other studies occupational therapy in college. She often talks about a nephew she's cajoling and badgering to continue his education.

Dolores is a long-time friend from my career. A few years after the loss of her husband of four-plus decades, she reconnected with a friend she had dated in college but had had no contact with for fifty years. A year after "circumstances and the Internet" brought them together, Joe and Dolores married. A year later she was diagnosed with uterine cancer and a year after that they learned her new husband had Alzheimer's.

She was successfully treated for cancer and became Joe's caregiver. He died five years after their wedding—certainly a sad story on the face of it. But hear her interpretation: "Both Joe and I experienced the five years we had together, including the time with Alzheimer's, as pure gift. We learned so much about love and patience."

Love and patience. They coexist as essential qualities of courage. Actually, anyone who has been married for a reasonable time knows one does not exist without the other. To accept these experiences as pure gift is courage in the face of suffering. We have no satisfactory answer for suffering in light of our belief in a loving, merciful God. But Dolores refused to let her losses be a hole that swallowed her.

And pure gift? How often in recent years have I heard that sentiment—from parents of developmentally impaired adult children, from friends who have suffered premature and sometimes grotesque loss of a child or a spouse? From a friend who watched her spouse disappear into the clouds of dementia. From parents of an adult child raked by incomprehensible betrayal. All made the courageous choice, the spiritual choice, not to let the event define them. All made the courageous choice to grow rather than wallow. The habits of their hearts trumped the rationalizations of their minds. As with Bill and Beverly and Dolores they too ignored the temptation to quit, refused to fall into the chasm they so precipitously walked along.

In the face of such unknowns ahead how do I hold steady? How I prepare is my spiritual challenge. I echo Rumi: "This self of ours is a part of hell. Only with the power of God can one overcome it."

But who is this God who effects our demise? And a loving God at that? Why does a God who loves us unconditionally permit such suffering? The paradox of the ages is reflected in a puzzling story about a good man who becomes a pawn in a game between God and a challenger minion named Satan. That would be Job. Poor beleaguered Job. For his loyalty and goodness, the loving God allows him to be hammered with all manner and sort of infliction and endure the endless speculation on why from friends and neighbors. Then, when good, long-suffering Job seeks an explanation God gives him a three-chapter lecture on God's creative power and majesty and a reminder that he, Job, is just a human, after all, incapable of comprehending the ways of God.

I don't find that at all satisfying and take no succor from the hair-splitting difference that God doesn't send us misery. But God does allow it. I know there is no answer to this paradox

So the search for Wisdom—God's feminine manifestation—continues. How much easier it would be to be a polytheist. Rather than struggling with why one true God allows evil, polytheists at least had the luxury of blaming misfortune and suffering on some cranky god they likely offended. "It's what that god does for a living, so let's placate him with a sacrificial lamb." But me, I believe in one God. Or, when struggling through one-way arguments, God's possibility.

In my pursuit of a loving God, I keep my eye on the prize of life's last stage— a good death.

Sometimes good fortune smiles on us. My sister, sixteen years my senior, died in her sleep. She left us before her time, at age seventy-two, and has been dearly missed. She was a good woman who loved generously and saw to the welfare of others as quickly as her own. When I got the phone call one dreary Sunday morning in March, I was stunned. I had no inkling. Just two weeks before, Sue and I went to see her. When we told our youngest daughter, who was about to marry and move offshore, that we were going, she asked if she could go with us. Then her older sister chimed in "what about me? I'd love to see Aunt Sally." So the four of us flew to my hometown for a long and wonderful weekend visit with her. She was her quick witted, loving self.

On news of her death, I quickly made plans to fly east and help my brother with the arrangements but first stopped to see Sue's mom before leaving for the airport. When I told Jane, then eighty-one years old, that Sally had died in her sleep, she exclaimed how wonderful that was.

Now, there I was, sick at heart at my sudden loss of a woman who had been often a surrogate mom and always a mentor, and my mother-in-law tells me how wonderful her death was? I was annoyed, a wounded boy wanting sympathy. It took some time before I saw that Jane was trying to shift my self-centered vantage to that of my sister: a woman who lived a generous life received a good death. A quick exit with no prolonged suffering.

And Jane wasn't finished. Her last lesson in life was how to die gracefully. As the diminishment called bone cancer steered her life to a close, this woman of deep and uncomplicated faith wished for three things:

- that her mind would remain sound,
- that she would keep her dignity, and
- that she would not be a burden.

Jane's mind remained good. She fretted about her episodic memory but faced it with her usual humor. "Did I know that once?" she'd ask when we'd talk of some event or fact. "Don't laugh," she'd say. "This could happen to you someday too." Memory problems or not, those of us who engaged her in some banter, challenged her politics, or took her on in cribbage or dominoes knew her mental acuity was vibrant despite endemic pain and increasing physical limitations.

She kept her dignity. A day or two before her death, with the oxygen tube in her nose, she pulled herself forward in her recliner and told me she was taking a walk. I knew better than to argue. A few steps away from her chair, both hands on the walker, she pulled her shoulders back. "I have to remember to stand straight," as she stretched out all five feet of her. A bit into the hallway one of the aides said, "Hi, Jane. Where are you going?" "To the end of my leash," she replied, referring to the long tube from her oxygen tank. I reminded her of her first use of a cane. "You told me you didn't need that thing to walk with, you just used it for balance," I teased. "Well, that's true," she insisted. Always the positive spin. She died in late March, but all that month, knowing the end was approaching, she would look out at the brown grass and barren trees and shrubs and say she was just waiting for the trees to bud and the grass to green. And the family of turkeys to parade by.

She was not a burden. Sue treasured multiple daily visits with her in her last months. Those who cared for her in her diminishment did so with gratitude. A hospice volunteer who played cribbage with her told me that being with Jane was "life altering. I learned something good about growing old." She didn't learn much about winning at cribbage, however.

The day she died, Sue and I found her struggling to eat her lunch. She had weakened alarmingly. She let us feed her, then told us she loved us. "I love you too," we each responded. It was the last coherent exchange we had.

She often said that she wanted God to take her home peacefully in her sleep and God did. She instructed all of us—in her uniquely toughminded way—not to grieve her death. So when we gathered for her funeral, we tried to honor her wishes by saying we were celebrating her life. But it was a ruse. Just a semantic ruse. We were mourning our loss. In time we recognized her victory. The habits of her heart overcame the rationalizations of her mind.

As with the hospice volunteer, I too learned something good about growing old, and I can only hope to carry it forward should I face the same condition. In growing old and dying I believe Jane reflected Romano Guardini's observation that

in old age something special happens to reality. Its hardness is softened by the experience of transitions. The view of things widens out. . . . Toward the end the whole comes again into view. As in autumn, when the leaves fall from the trees, the view expands, and one is conscious of a wide space.

Perhaps that expanding view is the portal to home.

4

Gratitude

Because all things have contributed to
your advancement, you should include
all things in your gratitude.

—Ralph Waldo Emerson

German Lutheran pastor Dietrich Bonhoeffer lived a moral imperative in the face of corrosive power. He lived life as an insightful theologian and died a martyr for his essential Christian beliefs, his adult life and career coinciding with the emergence of the Nazi State. He was quick to see it as the heart of evil and, unlike most churchmen of that era, stood in opposition to it.

When the Nazis coopted the local Lutheran churches to create the German Lutheran Federal Church in support of their political goals, and other churches either embraced the false promises of German exceptionalism or engaged in the self-preservation of silence, Bonhoeffer and others founded the Confessing Church. It stood in opposition to Aryan supremacy and its attendant racism and fostered solidarity with the Jews.

As a university professor Bonhoeffer used his teaching platform to challenge and condemn Nazism. He wrote extensively showing the conflict between National Socialism and Christian belief and in short time was denied his teaching position and then forbidden to do pastoral work. He continued his opposition, aligning himself with Hitler's political challengers, such as there were, and agonizing over the growing realization that assassinating the dictator was the only solution.

Bonhoeffer had traveled abroad, including living in London, New York, and Barcelona. He made many sympathetic friends along the way, friends who would have given him sanctuary as the Nazi regime tightened its grip. But he believed he belonged with his community in a time of extreme crisis. In 1943, ten years after he began to speak out against them and as a suspect in a plot to kill Hitler, the Nazis imprisoned him.

In late August 1944, knowing well the dire future he faced, he wrote to his friend Eberhard Bethge:

> I am so sure of God's guiding hand that I hope I shall always be kept in that certainty. You must never doubt that I'm traveling with gratitude and cheerfulness along the road where I'm being

led. My past life overflows with God's goodness, and my sins are covered by the forgiving love of Christ crucified. I'm most thankful for the people I have met, and I only hope that they never have to grieve about me, but that they too will always be certain of, and thankful for, God's mercy and forgiveness.

Seven months later the Nazis tried and executed him at a concentration camp. Within the month Hitler committed suicide and Nazi Germany collapsed.

That this man could travel "with gratitude and cheerfulness along the road where I'm being led" was the real exceptionalism, not the Nazi philosophy of Aryan supremacy. So sure was Bonhoeffer of God's love and Christ's spiritual embrace that he could look at the continuum of his life with "gratitude and cheerfulness." He shows us that gratitude is the difference maker. It steals the opposition's advantage and depletes the power of their adverse actions.

"Gratitude is the first movement of the spiritual life."

The phrase reverberated in my head and in my heart. It rewound itself again and again. Gratitude is the "first movement of the spiritual life"—a phrase cast off casually by a retreat director during a mini-retreat. I had already done several drafts of this chapter, so much of what he elaborated on rang true. It was "first movement" that was a new insight for me.

In reflecting on his seemingly offhand statement I thought of the first movement in a symphony or concerto where the composer sets up a tension between two contrasting themes. Analogously we all have things in life for which we are grateful, but sometimes they are hard to focus on amid our sufferings and setbacks. We know we should be grateful for life's gifts but succumb to the inevitable complaining that accompanies the human condition. So perhaps "first movement" involves reconciling the tension of finding gratitude within adversity.

This tension was made real with the recent death of a man who was a friend to all four of our children. He was a high-school classmate of our oldest son, teammate to both our sons, a high-school sweetheart to our oldest daughter, then engaged to one of her best friends in graduate school. Our youngest couldn't easily explain her affection. She certainly knew him but not as her sibs did. It seemed to be that "a friend of my sibs is a friend of mine." For the past twenty-four years he worked with our oldest at the resort on Nantucket. To three grandkids there he was "kick the ball" Johnny. He was simply always there, and then suddenly and unexpectedly no longer there.

The mourning was intense for us all, but especially for his loved ones and his contemporaries. He was one of the first of their own to die. The memorial service was packed and awash in tears. But oddly enough in the sea of sadness there were pools of gladness. As a teen and young man John had been a soccer star, a nearly unstoppable striker. A special testament to him was the presence of the defensive players from his school's archrival team. In their grief these now middle-aged people found gratitude for John's life, tears and solace in recalling stories and adventures through thirty five years, hugging friends rarely seen through the decades. And they were experiencing something we older folks have to come to know too well, that crying and laughing together isn't tension, it's therapy.

The word *movement* also indicates the establishment of a progression. As a first movement, gratitude becomes the starting point for spiritual awareness. Without it any effective exploration of the interior life or hope for a journey into the heart of God is unrealistic. It is only with the creation of this first movement that we can create the ensuing and related movements of spiritual growth.

How do we develop an awareness of the value of gratitude in ourselves? By recognizing that as the first movement in the spiritual life, gratitude is a virtue to be practiced, that it's a way of prayer, and that it can be nourished by wonder.

Gratitude Is a Virtue to Be Practiced

> *For gratitude is not only the greatest*
> *of virtues, but also the mother of all*
> *others.*
>
> —CICERO

One of our cultural legacies from the ancient Greeks is their belief that four characteristics were necessary to govern human behavior, to produce a decent life, and to mold a good society. They called them virtues and named them:

- justice—so that we will treat and be treated without bias,
- prudence—so that we will not rush to judgment, so that we will recognize what we should do and how we should act to be moral,
- courage—so that we will do what is right no matter what the circumstances, and
- temperance—so that we can achieve moderation in our use and consumption of all created things.

According to St. Paul these human virtues were nourished by the theological virtues that help us grasp and follow God's will. These are:

- faith—by which we believe in God and God's truth,

- hope— by which we desire union with God and eternal life, and
- charity—by which we live the great commandment to love God and neighbor.

We also try to live by virtues that stand in opposition to vices: chastity to overcome lust; temperance to restrain gluttony; charity to counter greed; diligence to balance laziness; patience to control quick temper; kindness to temper envy; humility to overcome pride.

Chivalry, the medieval code of conduct, held that virtues such as honor, loyalty, and generosity were essential to a knight's character.

Libraries full of books examine these various lists of virtues and offer testimony to their necessity in any code of behavior. Oddly enough gratitude is rarely found in lists of virtues. Yet Cicero, the Roman philosopher-politician, declared it the parent of all virtues. He used numerous examples to defend his belief and posed questions as relevant today as they were when he asked them over two thousand years ago:

- Do we really love our parents if we aren't grateful to them for what they did for us?
- Are we good citizens if we don't recollect the kindness received from our community?
- Isn't education an empty claim if we are ungrateful to our teachers and caregivers?

- Are we worthy of honors received if we are not grateful to God for them?
- Can friendship exist between ungrateful people? Isn't life empty without friendship?

Gratitude is the transcendent virtue. To be ungrateful, claimed this philosopher of old, "was inconsistent with the character of a virtuous man." Its lack compromises the other virtues, makes them difficult if not disingenuous to practice. Gratitude holds communities together. Without it we have no empathy, the ability to appreciate to one degree or another how a person feels or how our behaviors affect others.

David Steindl-Rast, a Benedictine monk, has authored numerous books on spirituality and travels the world delivering his message. He encourages us to look for the opportunity that always lurks in the present moment. To recognize the "wonderful riches of life" he suggests a simple three-step practice: stop, look, and go.

We need to slow down and stop so we can open all our senses and our hearts.

We need to look for the gift and the opportunity that each moment presents, to recognize life's wonderful riches and enjoy them.

We need to act on opportunity. Do whatever life offers us at that moment, mostly simply to enjoy it. And to reach out and help others "because nothing makes us more happy than when we are all happy." Gratitude is an engine of generosity. In understanding and appreciating our gifts, we become more willing to share. It's the opportunity to jettison the desire to acquire and ask what will make my life meaningful. Viktor Frankl, author of *Man's Search for Meaning,* a book transformative for so many of its readers, writes: "Being human always points, and is directed, to something or someone other than oneself. . . . The more one forgets himself—giving himself to a cause to serve and a person to love—the more human he is."

Standing with gratitude is especially beneficial in old age. We now have more opportunity to stop and to listen while sharing is more rewarding than accumulation. Dickinson's line from *Wild Nights*

> Futile—the winds—
> to a heart in port

is open to several interpretations. I prefer the sense that the wind is our friend, taking us to new and fulfilling realms, to harbors we've yet to see, both literal and metaphorical. So why spend these special years at anchor when we can set sail on both exterior and interior journeys?

Our lived reality tells us life is also a struggle. Life is fragile. With irritations, neglect, slights, aches, pains, drug side effects, and general slowing down, it's easy to be ill-tempered or surly as we age. Occasionally it seems that our mere presence is an annoyance to the generation behind us. The sometimes curt response from service people, the endless delays from a contractor or repair person, the indifference of some professionals to their older clients and patients seems to say that they are irritated with our slower responses or somehow threatened by wrinkles and white hair.

Getting perspective on such distractions, seeing beyond or around them, is a challenge. Yet the effort is rewarded. The spiritual practice of gratitude benefits our souls in the same way that ten thousand steps a day benefit our body or an active circle of friends benefits our emotions. It may seem hard, perhaps just easier to be a curmudgeon. But sociological and psychological research identifies and supports a laundry list of advantages. In comparison to curmudgeons, grateful people feel better emotionally, get sick less often, experience less stress, anxiety and depression, and take better care of their bodies. They even sleep better.

Grateful people tolerate loss well by seeing the bad in the context of the larger good—the joy of life. Fred Bronfman, a journalist who covered the wars in Southeast Asia, tells of a teenage boy working in the rice fields during the war. Even as the bombs fell he would sing while working. "I felt that although I might have to die," the boy told Bronfman, "it did not matter; that I just had to be happy in the midst of all the sadness of war, of the planes bombing us."

How he echoes John Adams: "Griefs upon griefs! Disappointments upon disappointments. What then? This is a gay, merry world, not withstanding."

How can we take this wonder drug that costs nothing and is easy to use, especially when there are areas of experience where gratitude comes easily. It's a spiritual exercise really, one that taps into our rich veins of experience and opportunity.

Tell your love story, and when you do, define it by your triumphs. It's too easy to wallow in the failures, to relive the conflicts, and to mourn the losses. Rather, revisit your successes, recall the decisions and events that gave purpose to your lives, those things you dreamed and schemed together to achieve. Celebrate them. They'll remind you just how much you have to be grateful for and help you focus on what gives meaning to your life.

Communicate with grandchildren. Better yet, if possible, plunk one on your lap and read a story. Or engage in a Wii game and watch the child collapse in gales of laughter at your ineptitude. I once sat at a dining room table, playing hangman with a three- or four-year-old grandson. He was at a stage when he really liked to win and actually struggled with losing. So I played lazily only to have him tell me after several games, "Grandpa, you're really horrible at this." Or take part in the key events of their lives. Grandparents Day at Walker School in a Chicago suburb was followed that evening by a youth soccer game and first communion the following day. At one point during the family celebration following the first communion our granddaughter gave me an unexpected hug around my middle and an unsolicited, "I love you, Grandpa." What a good weekend it was.

Keep family, extended and expanding, ever on your mind and in your heart. It's our blessing and our legacy. The public radio program *StoryCorps* undertook a massive collection effort over the 2015 Thanksgiving Holiday. It marshaled schoolchildren all over the country to interview their grandparents or other elders "to preserve the voices and stories of an entire generation of Americans, to collect its wisdom and archive it for the future."

In one interview a thirteen-year-old girl talked with her grandfather, who was dying of ALS. Under her simple questioning he acknowledged an understanding and acceptance of the reality of disease, offering us a poignant lesson in acceptance in the face of death. In the process he expressed gratitude for his life, gratitude for his spouse, his children, his grandchildren, his relatives, and his friends. "I'm grateful for you too, Jesse," he told the girl. Her voiced cracked out a soft thank you.

At the beginning of the week make a list of five or six things you're grateful for, then explore and reflect on one each following day. Perhaps even write down your thoughts in a notebook to revisit and reflect on. Remembering the good things of life will improve your mood.

Revisit your working life, searching for its rewards. Like most of us, my career was peppered with fits and starts, missteps and tumbles. On the whole, though, I was blessed with the opportunity and challenge of a career that grew into a calling; blessed with a wonderful group of dedicated fellow employees, so many of them now deceased; blessed with an environment that was the envy of any working stiff (except, perhaps, in February's snow and prairie winds); blessed with talented and committed authors, many of whom contributed significantly to my personal growth, the company's publishing legacy, and most important, to spreading God's love. How much they all taught me, some of which continues to drip from the distillery.

To practice caring is to practice gratitude. Everywhere we turn charity is needed, from global crises encompassing natural disasters, war, and refugees to local concerns involving poverty, the handicapped, and migrant workers. We can help, and we should help. But we doubt our effectiveness in the face of problems so massive, so complex, and so intractable. Giving money helps; helping another develop needed skills helps even more.

But if it is possible to meet God in another, perhaps effective help is not so difficult. Mother Teresa suggests that charity is also an attitude, a matter of "doing small things with great love for each other. Maybe a smile, maybe just thoughtfulness." We can't all be a Mother Teresa, but we can shift our focus from doing charity for something to doing it for somebody. The first is institutional; the second is person to person with the potential for personal enrichment.

Your memory is a logbook of people, events, and experiences. Wander through the index for a person or an event to delve into thoughtfully. As we live into the memory, a story that is both broader and deeper will likely emerge and we'll see something we hadn't noticed before.

This time of life offers us the opportunity to reflect with gratitude on those people who supported us and mentored us, who helped us find inner courage when it was needed most. I've been blessed with several, none more of a blessing than the man who gave me my first full time job out of college.

Tom is an ex-Marine who survived World War II in the Pacific where he was a navigator in a bomber squadron. He came home from the war, married, finished college, played a season or two in the minor leagues, and started a career in publishing. By the time he interviewed me for a job, he was the young owner of a growing publishing and printing company.

The interview went well, and he hired me. He not only trained me in the essentials of periodical publishing, but he became my mentor. He took a personal interest in me, complimented and criticized my work, and threw responsibility my way, confident I could handle it even when I felt the tremor of doubt. But there was no way I could let him down.

I worked for him for six years before moving on, but I never moved away from his tutelage. He always took my phone calls, always had time for a visit when I was back in town, always had keen advice. I learned from his example that mission came first, and that margin was the means to accomplish the mission. He put me on to the job that became my life's work and recommended me for it.

To say I am grateful to Tom is a vast understatement. He was the original good fortune of my career. We still exchange emails, mostly about college football, and we have lunch together once a year when I visit my hometown. We talk about mutual friends and family, publishing, current events, and he tells stories from his past. He's a joyful man, despite the difficult losses of age—his wife, Betty, died a dozen or more years ago, he lost a son to cancer about five years ago, and spinal stenosis has limited his mobility and deprived him of his beloved golf. Over the last few visits the relationship has shifted, and as he has repeated an observation that has sunk in only in retrospect. He talked glowingly about my career, leading to the comment, "It was a fortunate day when I hired you, Frankie." After all he had done for me, he was proud of and grateful to me. It's hard to express what that means. The teacher was grateful for the student; the teacher and the student were now friends and colleagues. His generosity of spirit awed me. But it was entirely in keeping with a man whose whole life was marked by good will and gratitude.

Another sure help in practicing gratitude is to keep upbeat friends close. I met Ed within the last five or six years. Skiing bought us together, a couple of old guys who still enjoy a day, although a short one, on the hill. To say nothing of the break for hot chocolate, a burger for lunch, and a beer before we head home. In the warm weather we bike, usually out to the state park and back. It's the good life, he tells me, reminding me of how lucky our generation has been. And he's so right.

One of fourteen children, he was born and spent his early life on a hardscrabble farm, then moved to a nearby town that was only a bit of an improvement. He went to college, married, had children, and enjoyed a career as a high-school teacher. He's always saying something to the effect, "Gosh, I mean I just have a wonderful life. Look at all the advantages I had and the wonderful things they've allowed me to enjoy. My life has been so much better than my mom and dad's. We're lucky to live when we do. It just couldn't be better." One of is favorite lines is "life is too short to drink cheap wine."

Take time to express gratitude to people in your life—spouse, kids, friends, mentors, public servants, men and women serving our country, anyone who is still around and helped along the way. Everyone feels better for the effort, an effort made near effortless by email.

It takes work not to become a curmudgeon, to be like the one cured leper of the ten who returned to thank Jesus. Gratitude is an antidote to the increasing constrictions of old age.

Gratitude Is a Way of Prayer

Gratitude therefore takes nothing for granted, is never unresponsive, is constantly awakening to new wonder and to praise of the goodness of God.

—Thomas Merton

Sometime in my early religious exposure a sister taught us that prayer consisted of three elements: praising God, thanking God, and asking God's blessing. Of course the last was the one we kids understood the best since it also covered asking God to grant some wish. How inviting it was to ask for model trains for Christmas or for a win by our favorite football team. The idea that prayer could be awareness of God's presence in the world around us, much less seeking union with this remote, favor-granting deity, was beyond the pale.

Sixty-five or more years later these three postures remain embedded in my bones. When all else fails, when the soul seems barren, just praise God, thank God, and ask for God's blessing.

Gratitude is deeply embedded in two of these postures: praise and thanksgiving. Remember Cat Stevens singing Eleanor Farjeron's hymn of praise?

> Morning has broken like the first morning
> Blackbird has spoken like the first bird
> Praise for the singing, praise for the
>   morning
> Praise for them springing fresh from the
>   Word

It's a contemporary prayer of gratitude reminding us to wake daily in thanksgiving for abundance—for the rains, for the sunlight, for the dewfall, for the wet garden. Indeed, it reminds us to praise God's "re-creation of every new day."

It seems to take its inspiration from the book of Daniel with its joyful "Song of the Three Young Men." This hymn reminds us that no matter how dire our circumstances or diminished our capacities, our first response should be to recognize our good fortune and thank

God for it. The hymn is the culmination of a colorful
Old Testament story of power, vengeance, intrigue, and
integrity. The setting was ancient Babylon when King
Nebuchadnezzar had a golden statue built for all to fall
down and worship at his command.

When three exiled Jews—Shadrach, Meshach, and
Abednego—who are employed in the king's bureaucracy,
refuse to honor false gods, the king has them bound and
thrown into a fiery furnace as punishment for their dis
obedience and disrespect. He has his strongest soldiers
bind them so they can't escape and has the fire stoked to
seven times its normal heat. Once in the furnace the three
are untouched and begin their canticle as an angel of the
Lord drives the flames away while blowing in on them "a
coolness such as wind and dew will bring." Their hymn
is at first one of praise, blessing Yahweh "in the vault of
heaven, exalted and gloried above all else forever."

It quickly slides into one of gratitude for God's power,
and they bless God for "all things the Lord has made."
Through nearly forty verses we hear gratitude enumer-
ated for waters, the sun and moon, showers and dews,
stars in the heavens, frost and cold, nights and days, lightning and clouds, mountains and hills, to list but a few.
They end the song by blessing the "God of gods, praise
him and give him thanks, for his love is everlasting." In
the face of the miracle Nebuchadnezzar has no choice but
to order them out of the furnace, at which point he too

proclaims, "Blessed be the God of Shadrach, Meshach, and Abednego."

It's one of those bible stories I'd long forgotten until a friend sent me back to it as a reminder of how the hymn connects us with nature. The three young men tell us to this day that God's hand is in our lives and in all that we depend on for life.

As the slings of arrows of aging diminish us in so many ways, the three young men remind us to first remember all the good things that surround us.

In my near-daily walks I am cheered by the thoughts of loved ones, mentors and friends, acquaintances and work associates, often reminded of what they did for me, what they taught me, how they expanded my worldview. When my mind wanders down weird ways, I seem to be always able to bring it back by thinking of a specific person and finding a reason to be thankful to or for that person. As an exercise in appreciation, I suppose my feeling that it is also prayer is open to challenge. But then, my path to God has been anything but unchallenged.

Gratitude Is Nourished by Wonder

> *Life without wonder is not worth living. What we lack is not a will to believe but a will to wonder.*
>
> —Rabbi Abraham Heschel

To cradle a sleeping newborn child in your arms is to experience wonder.

To spot a double rainbow after a summer downpour is to experience wonder.

To feel the giddiness of the northern lights on one of their rare appearances in our latitude is to experience wonder.

To listen to a world-class orchestra interpret Bruckner's Eighth Symphony is to experience wonder.

To experience wonder is to experience gratitude—to be grateful for both nature's gifts and human accomplishments. Grateful for this state of rapture called life.

Dusk dissipates quickly at the bottom of the Grand Canyon in early November, and the density of the darkness surprises in the absence of artificial light. Our eyes adjust, and the stars seem to quickly pop and penetrate the inky black sky. Puffy clouds drift past the gibbous moon, alternately shrouding and admitting its soft light. There is no glow of refracted human light here. No sounds of modern settlement either. Just the rumble of the Colorado River a few hundred yards away, the intermittent chatter of campers, and the occasional braying of mules.

I'm in awe, reluctant to give it up and crawl into my bunk at one of the Phantom Ranch cabins. The fourteen-mile trek down the north rim of the canyon was amazing, the natural beauty living up to every morsel of its reputation, its "see forever" clarity revealing layer upon layer of unfolding landscapes. Now comes the night, several more hours of wonder before sleep and an early morning departure for the eleven-mile ascent up the south rim.

Before retreating from the night chill for my heavily blanketed bunk, I think this must be what it was like for ancient civilizations. How astute they were in gazing at this sky and seeing patterns and outlines they named after familiar earthly objects and animals. I think of one of those wonderful television specials on the cosmos that asked how many stars were in the universe. They lost me halfway through the means of calculation, but the answer was startling. It was a number with no name, only a description—a two followed by twenty-two zeros. Write that number out on a piece of paper. It's as long as this sentence. Well, maybe a few characters shorter. The ancients knew none of this. They knew only that the night sky was so massive, so pervasive, so full of pinpoints of light, and so powerful that it must have some influence, even dominance, in their lives. By naming its parts they organized the sky, became familiar with it, and gained a small measure of control.

I mumble a prayer of thanks for such an opportunity; for friends who organized this self-guided trek and invited me to join them; for the perfect weather; for health good enough for such a trip; for a touch of the daft to do it at our age, all of us official seniors; for Joyce, whose Camino planted the seed and launched me on a decade of reaping rich rewards of walking and trekking. Then there were the two wives who greeted us with cold beer on top of the south rim that hot afternoon.

Wonder begets gratitude begets wonder begets gratitude begets a virtuous circle.

We have to be attuned to the opportunities for wonder. The impressive achievements of modernity—from ease and quickness of travel to the warmth and comfort of our dwellings, from the tools that facilitate our work to the endless diversions that fill our leisure hours—mislead us. They tell us that we're the source of our gratification, suck us into the emptiness of hubris. That is, until we hold a newborn baby in our arms, witness a rainbow, listen to a symphony, or gaze at the night sky.

The practice of gratitude involves looking back over our lives from a new vantage point. Time no longer seems endless. We've learned something from our mistakes. We can more quickly separate the wheat from the chaff. We discover that life's little stories were the building blocks of our journey.

I don't know for certain when the ritual started. Very likely in the early winter of 1948 as I was preparing for my first communion at Midnight Mass that Christmas.

It involved a visit to McManus and Riley men's store for my first suit—a white one with short pants.

It was the first of numerous trips to this long-gone business located on the North Side of the first block of State Street in Albany, New York, within sight of the State Capitol at the top of the hill. "Correct Attire for Gentlemen and Boys" went the store's slogan. It was an era when even a boy needed a proper suit.

So, driven by my growth spurts, my mom would steal a Saturday morning with the neighborhood kids from me. Reluctantly I'd ride the bus downtown with her, walk the short distance from the State and Pearl Street stop to the store, and ride the elevator to an upper floor that housed the boys' department. There a familiar gentleman would greet my mom by name and offer his help. On the wall was a rack of boys' suits from small to large and a special section for husky. And a rack of small white suits in an obscure section—McManus and Riley, by virtue of its name, had a brisk business in first communion suits. Shifting from foot to foot, looking out the windows, and generally wanting to be with my buddies, I'd try on jackets and pants to the soft-spoken cadence of phrases like "won't show the dirt," "moderately priced," "good quality," "room to grow" and "alterations included."

Once a suit was agreed on, a tailor would emerge from some mysterious recess in the store, cloth tape-measure draped around his neck, pins in his lapels (yes, he too wore a suit), and a piece of soap with a shaved edge in his hand. I'd stand on a chair, and he'd measure and mark the sleeves and pant legs, then waist and crotch. "The suit will be ready for pickup on Tuesday," he'd say.

By the time I was thirteen years old and had a paper route and a handful of lawn-mowing customers, my mom and dad made it clear that purchasing clothes was now my responsibility. So began the savings account and a new Christmas and birthday strategy. No more toys. Now I wanted sweaters and shirts as a hedge against having to buy all my clothes. As I got into high school, I began to make the suit purchase by myself. Along with chinos and jeans, ties and shirts, and socks and underwear. Such responsibility may seem harsh these days, but such norms encouraged self-reliance in the neighborhood of my youth.

This was an era when men and women dressed "properly" for nearly all occasions, from baseball games to church. Especially church. My dad was a tradesman who set type for the local newspapers for fifty-six years, having started his apprenticeship at fourteen. He wore a suit, tie, and fedora to church every Sunday. All the dads in the neighborhood did. Ken's dad, a school principal, did. Fran's dad, a postal worker, did. Joe's dad, a banker, did. Ed's dad, a car salesman, did. Little Mike's dad, the synagogue custodian, did. I can't speak with any accuracy about the moms other than that they too "dressed up." You could tell by the hats, the millinery kind. I'd see them all walking to and from St. James on Sunday morning.

I'd also see the dozen or so Jewish men in the neighborhood attired the same way as they walked to evening prayer in the synagogue at the head of Federal Street, practically in my backyard. Sometimes they would interrupt one of our street ball games and ask one of us to go into the sanctuary to turn on the lights. I'd learn years later that I was a *shabbat goy,* a gentile asked to do certain tasks that the Torah forbade a pious Jew.

My high school required jackets and ties in all classrooms, a rule we followed with cavalier indifference. I probably used the same black knit tie for four years. We all left battered sports coats in our lockers till they showed three inches of shirtsleeve and were too tight to button. It was our little rebellion that said "you can insist that we dress as gentlemen, but we'll show you that we're still teenage boys."

I bought my last suit at McManus and Riley when I was eighteen and a senior in high school—a slim cut, three-button roll, dark brown and black, the colors distinguished by a very subtle wale. When I went for a job interview around graduation time, the personnel director invited me to sit down with the comment, "Nice suit, young man." Important lesson applied.

I got the job, but it would last for only the summer, a brief flirtation with working for several years and delaying my education and saving some money for it. The idea was summarily squashed when my older sister, whom I dearly loved and respected, told me "no way." I was going to college then, no delays. She used a few words for emphasis that I'd never heard her use before. But then, she had watched my two older brothers impatiently slip into the Army and Marines, one of them before he finished high school. Her insistence that I to go to school shorted me on tuition money, but I was a day-hop student who found work after classes. And I had a nice suit.

In 1959 the jacket and tie was ubiquitous, a near universal dress code, a generations-old expectation. Learning to present a good personal appearance was an important discipline of growing up. My dad taught me how to tie a Windsor knot, how to fold and hang up my clothes, and made sure I had a razor when the time came. It was a sturdy, silver, double-edged device that took Gillette Blue Blades. It couldn't have been anything else—pop was a regular Friday-night-fights fan. He also once advised me on the best brand of tools to buy.

When my brother Don, twelve years my senior, came back from the Marine Corps in 1953, he showed me how to make a bed tight enough to bounce a quarter off it. More useful, he taught me to press my pants and shine my shoes. Spit-shine them for that matter. I could see my reflection in the buffed toe cap. "The Clothes Make the Man," ran one of the popular advertisements of the day. Since we were beginning to discover girls, we felt it probably applied to boys too.

Although these were significant lessons for a teenage boy, they were also family ritual, like my dad accompanying each of his kids for our first vote.

Men could make a respectable living selling clothes. The dad of one of my schoolmates was a familiar face in menswear at a downtown department store. The salesmen did it by building relationships through service and satisfaction. For about a year while in college I sold men's clothing in the local Montgomery Wards. The full-time salesmen, working on salary and commission, were not to be trifled with. They were adept at picking out the most promising shoppers on the floor—often women shopping for their husbands—and getting to them before we few part-timers had a chance. For them, it was a matter of a roof over their head and food on the table. For us, it was just tuition and date money.

It all started to unravel during the 1960s, that beautifully traumatic decade that would quake societal foundations and shake behavioral codes violently. Some codes were silly and just as well jettisoned. But I wonder about the dress code. Its erosion ultimately led to leisure suits, and how could that have been a good thing?

The changing code was often confusing. In the mid-
seventies I interviewed a manager of the Peninsula Hotel
in Hong Kong for a travel piece. At that time high tea in
the lobby of this elegant hotel called for jacket and tie.
But it had become problematic. She gave up enforcing
it when a waiter asked a guest wearing blue jeans and a
sport shirt to leave. He was Persian Gulf royalty and not
in the least bit happy at being singled out for dismissal.

Like most of my generation I embraced casual wear,
even in the workplace and church. As with most changing codes, some folks go to extremes. Although I wear a
jacket to church only for weddings, funerals, and maybe
Christmas and Easter, I find some church-going attire
distracting, maybe even lacking reverence. Social norms
still make statements about our values.

Are these just easily dismissed musings of an aging
man who embraced and/or adapted to his share of
changes over the decades? Of course. But it is also an
exercise in living out of my memories. It's an exploration of what time has to tell me. Not as navel gazing
but as a means of understanding who I am. It's a kind of
therapeutic nostalgia—this exploration of the people,
events, and customs that shaped us, that helped direct
the choices we would make, that helped establish the
habits of our hearts.

When I engage in such reflection, I often land in a
pool of gratitude. For parents with the wisdom to impart

self-reliance and respect for things that take hard work to earn; for a sibling with the courage to face down an eighteen-year old with money in his pocket and the desire to put education on hold; for a brother with the generosity to impart some of the discipline of personal care.

And they are only the hull and keel for this creaking boat. The deck, sails, and rigging are a woman who agreed to share her life with me, children who grew up to become good people and loving parents, and a handful of mentors and supporters who saw some promise in me that I hardly saw myself. From them all I learned to chart the course and take the helm.

After all, exploring gratitude becomes a habit of the heart. A habit that fosters the courage to live the last act, the final inning, as completely as possible.

5

Acceptance

*This is the day that the Lord has
made: let us rejoice and be glad in it.*

PSALM 118:24

few Christmases ago, our daughter Sally and
her family gave me a genealogy kit. It identifies lineage by running a DNA saliva test. I took a swab
as instructed and mailed it in with the fond hope that I
would find out I was Italian. You see, Italian families were
part of the tapestry of my youth. Then, after college I
spent several months in Italy, met my lifelong love there,
and returned on several occasions. As a result:

- I love Italy and the Italians.
- I love their passion for living and their humor.
- I love their rugged countryside and seascapes.
- I love the way they gather in the evenings in cafes
  to gossip over Campari or a coffee and maybe a
  sweet, or to stroll in their *piazzas*.

- I love their gift for animated conversation.
- I love their wine and their food.

When the test results came back I was a tad disappointed to learn I was a Celt, probably going back to Eastern Europe. I wasn't surprised. The little bit of genealogy I once dabbled in revealed a tree full of McGaughans, Mc-Closkeys, Devaneys, Murphys, Callahans, and Harrigans. So I accepted the inevitable. After all, Irish families were part of the tapestry of my youth and my lifelong love is Irish—mostly. And our visit there was one to remember. As with Italy,

- I love Ireland and the Irish.
- I love their passion for living and their humor.
- I love their rugged countryside and seascapes.
- I love the way they gather in the evenings in the pubs in their villages and neighborhoods for a pint and often spontaneous music.
- I love their gift for animated conversation.
- I love their whiskey.

The food? Well, clear advantage here to the Italians.

The acceptances necessary later in life are not so trivial. If they were, cosmetic surgeons would be out of work and eighty-somethings would give up their driver's licenses without such a fuss.

In a time of steady diminishment, accepting and dealing with it is a source of constant contemplation, a key spiritual practice of aging, another aspect of the exam ined life. Author Gene Hemrick tells us that the virtue in acceptance is found in surrendering to the truth of the matter rather than pretending it doesn't exist. We have to determine and accept the reality of what is if we hope to deal with it effectively   whether we hope to change it, draw strength from it, or submit to it, if necessary.

I struggle to accept my diminishments, alternately smug after a day of skiing or biking, disconsolate when seemingly unearned fatigue saps my interest or some medical procedure wreaks havoc with my energy. I tell myself to engage them willingly so I can find the sweet spot in my decline and make the most of it, to understand that it's folly to pretend they are not happening, folly not to push back against them. It raises the quandary of accepting that I am no longer the person I once was while not forgetting that other person who is all too real in my head and heart—that twenty-two-year-old or thirty-year-old residing in atrophying housing.

What does the truth of the matter look like?

My friend Mark is a recovering alcoholic. To hear him tell it, he spent thirty years hiding in a bottle or a glass. He would never be in recovery if he had not recognized and accepted his addiction. Through a long and patience-testing process, he surrendered to "the truth of the matter" and his acceptance of it gave him the wherewithal to engage the twelve steps.

On the other hand, one of my family members has been an addict for nearly as long. He's experienced numerous family interventions, loss of his trade, failure of two marriages, and the alienation of his adult children. He's been arrested, and he has taken part in both inpatient and outpatient treatments. He must know he's an addict. But he continues on the same path. Somehow he has failed to surrender to the truth of the matter, to accept that he is an addict.

The truth of the matter can be slow to emerge and challenging to reconcile. Ken has had heart problems for a number of years that have been treated with stents and a defibrillator. His health has been further compromised by back problems for which he has had extensive treatments. A suspected but elusive spinal leak has caused debilitating headaches that are relieved only by lying down. Tests and treatment over a four-year period have been ineffective. He reluctantly parses his out-of-bed time knowing that the onset of a headache concurs with his rising. The combination of problems has sapped his energy and he spends about 90 percent of his time in bed. The reality of these limitations, in Ken's words, is "a shortened lifecycle."

He still pursues engagement—reading extensively and listening to recorded books, talking on the phone with family and friends, getting himself up and into a chair to welcome visitors. He even occasionally joins a group of eight or ten men who meet for lunch a couple of times a week. He really enjoys the gatherings, especially the political conversations, but this hour or so bit of pleasure puts him in bed for the rest of the day.

A news junkie and history buff, he occasionally invites a few friends to the house for coffee and always lively conversation. An unabashed liberal, he relishes other points of view.

For Audrey—they've been married for fifty-nine years—the truth of the matter is the necessity to focus on Ken's needs first. The ordinary things she might do for family or friends or herself are put aside until his needs are met. "Helping Ken is what my life is now about," she says without a trace of bitterness or rancor. They clearly miss the capability to go out together for something to eat, to see a movie, to attend a performance, or to hear a speaker. But this is disappointment not acrimony. It's acceptance.

Both Ken and Audrey struggle with "things will get better." Ken accepts that they will not. Audrey prods, offering encouragement to pursue another avenue on the chance that they *will* get better. "My job has been to fix things," she says good-naturedly. "I think we have to keep trying."

"I know what he can do," she says emphatically.

"I know what I can't do," he says with equal emphasis.

He then smiles as he says, "You see where we are on this." Then he quickly points out how grateful he is for her care and concern as he has lost ground.

Ken turns to his faith to help accept his condition, but "I struggle with what God's will is." He struggles with why his deterioration would be thought of as God's will. To be told that "this is God's will" offers him no comfort. Yet he finds strength as he turns to God in prayer. "I pray in the morning for God to help me through the day. I pray at night in gratitude for what I've been given and to help me through the night."

Some acceptances are general, relevant to us all, while others are more personal. In the broad stroke view I find three acceptances helpful to reflect on: our story, our brokenness, and dealing adequately with death.

Accept our story. We need to accept our story while understanding that it is not yet finished. Looking back reflectively gives us strength to move on. We have an ending to write, a satisfactory closure to complete. The ending is a matter of peace of mind. It's worth repeating from an earlier chapter that our story is not just a fact-based recall of events, accomplishments, failures, growth, or diminishment. It is also about recognizing an arc of nourishment, a leading theme that fed the multiple phases of our past, a storyline that fostered our growth and now

helps us understand who we are. Theologian Leonard
Baillas tells us that "the supreme achievement of the self
is to find an insight that connects together the events,
dreams, and relationships that make up our existence."
Searching for that insight, that storyline, is an exercise
is critical self-reflection.

Completing our story is our opportunity to explore
deep truths or what the liberal arts once referred to as
the eternal verities, those truths that make us human,
that lead to behaviors we know are right. We assume
them to be part and parcel of the human psyche. They
are useful abstractions that we extract from the human
experience; for example, the common understanding
that there is good and there is evil, and that love con-
quers hate. They are truths that transcend cultures.

Exploring deep truths involves reflecting on how
experiences of love, compassion, hope, joy, and truth
have shaped our story. What if we were to take on one
of these truths and sit with it in the early morning light
with a cup of coffee? For example, think about how
compassion fit into our story and what its presence will
be in the days ahead. Will the gift of time afford us the
opportunity to see to someone else's welfare? Or in our
experiences of love did we truly transcend self-interest
to place the needs of others first? Do we recognize love
as the source of happiness? Did we seize our moments
of joy? Did we even recognize them?

We may find that we pursued false promises and believed in false gods, that who we are should not be reflective of what we have. But now different opportunities are revealed. We have the chance and the challenge to convert a leading theme from a negative to a positive. Dusk, after all, brings the brilliance of the evening star, a prelude to darkness, but a darkness punctured by millions of stars, perhaps even revealing the Northern Lights.

Perhaps such an exercise will help us grasp that we are still on the journey to discover and become the person God intended us to be. Our life story is largely behind us. Perhaps it has even reached its narrative climax, but our denouement can be a very powerful experience. It begins by acknowledging that we have an inner life that needs tending. In that tending we will compose our last chapter.

Accept our brokenness. We don't hear much about Herman Hesse anymore, but in the sixties and seventies this early twentieth-century German author and Nobel Laureate experienced a revival. Perhaps it was because his pacifism spoke to the futility and disgraces of the Vietnam war. Perhaps his interest in the religions of Asia pointed to an antidote for those who felt that Christianity had failed through the traumas of the twentieth century. Perhaps it was because one of his main characters, Siddhartha, reflected the angst of the age.

Whatever the reasons, Hesse's writings, particularly *Siddhartha* and *Steppenwolf*, strike me as wisdom literature. In *Siddhartha* Hesse writes:

> Everything that exists is good—death as well as life, sin as well as holiness, folly as well as wisdom. Everything is necessary; everything needs only my agreement, my assent, my loving understanding; then all is well with me and nothing can harm me.

To extrapolate a bit, brokenness makes us whole; brokenness is a reflection of the good of our lives.

Our failures contribute to our brokenness. We are encouraged not to be afraid of failures, that if we don't fail we are not trying. We use failure as a measure of our character. Do we claim we are victims or shift the blame to someone else when we fail? Or do we shake it off, accept our responsibility, and keep on keeping on?

I accept the truth of that when the results of the failure are mine alone. But what of the failures that hurt others? The failures that show we have let others down? The failures by which we have violated our integrity? There's a laundry list of those mistakes and bad judgments. We have no option but to accept them, forgive them, be kind to them, use them to help make us whole.

Our losses contribute to our brokenness. And it starts early. Losses in which we fail to grasp the nature of death because we are immortal at that age: the young history teacher who is replaced two thirds of the way through our sophomore year and dies within weeks; the grade school and high school classmate who dies of leukemia before she is twenty-one; the ageless uncle who is no longer there to tease and encourage.

When the awareness of death's permanence does dawn, it dawns hard. Only a few months out of college, a close friend died. We had known each other since early grade school and shared the intensity and excitement of our coming-of-age years. Paul was brilliant, funny, and handsome. I was traveling when my folks' letter told of his death while driving through a mountain pass in a heavy rain. I cried on the Spanish Steps. He had not yet cast his first vote.

Just a few months before, after graduation in the spring of 1963, he had moved into the Colorado Rockies for a summer geology internship. I bolted for Europe to spread youthful wings. We both took modest chances. Through all the ensuing years these questions have surfaced: Why did Paul die? Why did he go off the road in the rain while I survived bobbing around in a hurricane on a decrepit Yugoslavian freighter?

Paul pursues me, visiting occasionally in a vivid, always-the-same dream. His youthful self shows up at some event and I ask, "Where the heck have you been?" But I encounter only a quiet Paul through the distortion of old glass. I wake to the loss of shared lives. I never got to give him that "full report" he expected on Europe. He would have loved Sue and after meeting her would have said, "No way, Cunningham. How did you pull this one off?"

And he was only the beginning of the inevitable losses that sadden the passage of time—parents, siblings, friends, workmates, and saddest of all, children of friends, children lost out of sequence.

Sometimes circumstances demand an epic acceptance. I met Henri, a shrimper in the Gulf of Mexico, after Hurricane Katrina had destroyed his home and his village. He's a cinder block of a man, about 5 feet 7 inches or so, around 250 pounds. Bump into him and you bounce. His hands were worn and beaten from five decades of shrimping and boat building, his sun-darkened face deeply lined from years of days on the open water. He moved purposefully, knowing how to pace himself and conserve his battered body. He spoke with the cadence and distinctive dialect of his own finger of the Mississippi River delta, a place called Delacroix. It was home for all of his sixty-three years before Katrina put him and his wife on a docked cruise ship and then into a FEMA trailer on a lot east of New Orleans that belonged to one of his children.

After some of us spent a day helping him refit and expand tool bins on trailers that would carry tools to the crews that were gutting homes ravaged by flood, mold, and vermin, he invited us to see the shrimp boat he and a lifelong friend had built. We drove to Delacroix in the late afternoon. On the way he offered us nearly a house-by-building view of what had been, pointing repeatedly to spots where family, cousins, in-laws, and lifelong friends once had homes and jobs. Two homes remained out of all the houses, shops, churches, and commercial buildings in this community of one thousand strung out along Terra Boeuf bayou. One stood cabled and turn-buckled to fourteen-foot concrete stilts set deep in the ground. The other stood stark amid debris and foliage made ghostly by the saltwater surge. Henri called it the "angel spot." Inexplicably, the house had withstood Katrina, and then Rita, as it had withstood Betsy four decades ago.

Shortly he directed me to stop at a cement pad that had once held his home. There this hardened man, husband and father of three, grandfather to a gaggle and great-grandfather of one, cried softly. "It's a hard pill to swallow," was all he could say. I could offer scant succor. Henri, his community now scattered around the country, mourned not just the loss of his house, but the possible loss of a way of life that centered on taking a living from the sea, of neighbors helping neighbors whenever needed, of a community shaped by networks of extended families.

His shrimp boat had survived in a safe harbor, now a white and blue-trimmed anomaly amid the flotsam. A few crab pots hung over the side. He pulled them, smiling at the handful of crabs in each, telling us how good they were when boiled with vegetables, shrimp, spices, and sausage for community gatherings. "What about shrimping? Can you go back out?" I asked. "No infrastructure," he replied. No ready fuel, no icehouses for storage, no brokers for buying, no truckers for transporting. His work was now limited to being the carpenter in a tent city, awaiting an uncertain future.

He spoke lovingly of his nearby family, especially his grandkids. "They're on the upside of life. I'm on the downside," he said with a forlorn realism. Henri was accepting and dealing with his losses, but I was sinking in the futility of the little help we offered. I thought I could handle such wreckage, having lost a home in a super typhoon in the tropical Pacific; and I had reported for weeks on human duress following the evacuation of Vietnamese refugees in 1975. But I was young then. Ashamedly, I now ached to leave, afraid to tussle with the meaning of such loss at this stage of our lives.

In our brief acquaintance over a couple of days of building tool bins, I found a man of resigned acceptance but one who was never personally broken. Set back on his heels for sure. Afraid he would never return to Dela-croix. "The destruction was too thorough." But he was a resourceful and experienced man who knew how to work. A decade on, Delacroix has been largely rebuilt—on stilts—and I have little doubt that Henri made his way home. Given any chance to return home, he would do so.

I believe Hesse is right that this is all part of the hu-man condition, a measure of an overarching good. What choice do we have but to give our assent, our agreement? What mess do we create if we do not? Refusal is denial. But our loving understanding? I have to work on that one even though I know that brokenness is a path to redemption.

Mary Craig reminds us that the strength in brokenness is freedom: "Seizing hold of that strength, choosing to face an uncertain future with hope rather than immerse oneself in the wreckage of one's past is the one impor-tant freedom we have."

Accept the need to reconsider our cultural norms for death. Actuaries estimate that I'll live about eleven more years and Sue will live thirteen. I'll be eighty-six then and can expect to live another five-and-a-half years. That will take me past ninety-one and grant me the expectation of four more years from there. Sue fares even better. And so goes the statistical game. We just may never die, so why talk about it? Why try to prepare for such a distant inevitability?

My grandfather's generation had a life expectancy of forty-five years. My dad's generation added three more. Those of us born in 1941 could expect to live until age sixty-two. And the odds improved with time. Better living conditions, safer diets, and the achievements of modern medicine have given us longer and better lives indeed. Even when we are seriously ill there's a medical solution, or the hope of a solution, or the hope for an experimental therapy, so much so that we too often pursue extreme or marginally valuable treatments that diminish the quality of our lives. So powerful is the desire to live that we detour around the reality of impermanence and fail to discuss how far we want to go to avoid the inevitable, to consider the price we are willing to pay for a few more tomorrows.

When it comes to end of life, those in our cohort walk a fine line between submission and fighting on as we try to find the truth of the matter. Can we accept our diminishments without losing sight of who we are at heart? Remember Bill of an earlier chapter? He got it when he said: "I do not and will not define myself by my illnesses. I'm not a cancer victim or survivor. I'm a child of God and take that as my identity. I look to see what's ahead, not what's over."

We don't talk about dying much. Not in any meaning-ful way. We don't talk about it with our adult children. It's uncomfortable. It just doesn't seem imminent. Sta-tistically, it is not. We exercise a denial driven by our compulsion to live abetted by modern medicine's power to delay the one certainty of being alive: Death.

So why try to determine what we would like at the end of life? Because time left concentrates the mind. Because life is fragile. Because the end can come quickly and surprisingly. Because the details and choices of our final time can be taken out of our hands by well-intentioned, highly competent professionals whose job is to keep us alive. And we may not like those results. What could be a more appropriate spiritual exercise than thinking prayerfully and carefully about how we want our lives to end? What will be our priorities given the potentially difficult choices involved in ongoing care? When does enough become enough? When does the now take precedence over an unsure and potentially debilitated future?

My dad experienced a prolonged and painful death. He was a proud ex-Marine who fought death all the way, living in severe debilitation for almost two years. He even let his leg be amputated in the faint hope it would give him more time. On his deathbed he told my brother, "Don't let me go." My mom, on the other hand, suffered physical and mental diminishments that led to a decision for hospice care at a reasonable time. Her last months were peaceful and relatively free of suffering.

Although our longevity is stretched more and more, the desire for it isn't new. In Roman mythology the horses of the night pulled the chariots of time. The poet Ovid pleaded, "Run slowly, slowly, horses of the night." He wanted time to creep so he could be with his lover longer. Seduced by life and fearing death, we too try to slow the horses of the night.

Beowulf was one of dozens of books I wanted to read in retirement. And I did. As I was sitting in my son's living room early one morning he brought me some coffee and asked, "What other high-school classics are you going to read?" And therein lay the problem. We read and are turned off by such books at a time when we lack the experience to understand their message. And *Beowulf* expresses many truths, among them the lesson that life's accumulations, conquests, and achievements become meaningless when "the killer stalks." As we wait for the end, we would give it all back for more time.

Bargain and pray though we may, we soon enough have to accept our ultimate limit. We don't win a battle with death. We only win with a peaceful death.

When the Dalai Lama was asked if he feared death, he replied, "It's just a change of clothes." That's acceptance. Or as Henri Nouwen told Chicago's beloved Cardinal Bernardin, "People of faith who believe that death is the transition from this life to life eternal should see it as a friend." That's quite a challenge when we realize we not only accept our friends, we welcome them.

The decline that most of us experience gradually through adulthood accelerates alarmingly, pointing to a rapid transition on this leg of the journey. It will be transition from activity to passivity and to the realization that some day, like an increasing number of friends, I will become a heart in port, no longer able to harness the winds.

As for personal acceptances, what do they look like for this well-established senior?

I accept who I am, who I've become on this downhill part of my long walk. But I know I have more to discover, that I can make more out of life. I embrace my seventy-five years. I arrived here through life's slings and arrows and don't want to be a twenty-something again.

I accept the diminishment of possibilities. I know of rooms whose doors will no longer open for me, recognize streams whose ice will never thaw, embers that will never again flare. I don't need to fulfill my fantasy to live in Tuscany for a year but will pursue a visit with any of my kids or grandkids this weekend. Fine dining has little appeal, but I won't miss breakfast with Sue on Saturday morning. Preferably at Nemos or the Phoenix, where they know our names. I don't care if I cross an ocean, but I revel in a Lake Michigan sunset. It's not that the broader world no longer interests me. It does. But I feel my focus slowly narrowing to family, friends, and small pleasures.

I accept, too, that I am a skeptical person of faith. I pursue this God that science and technology cannot find, but whom the poets and mystics sense and allude to. I look for the signs. I take heart from Guardini's reminder in *Learning the Virtues* that we did not construct our own existence but received it. But from where? Is it "from the blind course of nature, the senselessness of chance, the malice of a demon—or from the pure wisdom and love of God." I opt for God's probability and the deep joy when belief blooms.

I accept that I am piously impaired, that the usual forms of prayer and other spiritual exercises leave me mostly empty, that my desire to be a spiritual person is largely a triumph of hope over experience. So I look for God's presence in creation and relationships.

I hear no still small voice, yet I feel a still, small voice. What moved me to undertake the Camino de Santiago? Oh, I can trace the genesis of the idea. But what moved me? What made me put one foot in front of another? Inspiration, we say. But isn't inspiration an invasion by the Spirit?

Inherent in acceptance is the need to wait. By waiting I mean simply being. As we age we move from activity to being, from the doer of actions to the receiver of actions. This can be terrifying in a world that measures human worth and meaning solely by activity and achievement. When we become passive, the object of activity, our value is reduced. As passives in a frantically active world we can become burdens, ultimately even "patients" relegated to senior living facilities, some of which are little more than warehouses. We spent the first years of life passively, the object of the activity of others, and we strove for the activity of independence. But the passivity of old age is less than inviting. It involves giving up mobility and independence without the promise of the love and nurture we likely had as infants and children.

As Dylan Thomas tells us in his most famous lines:

> Do not go gentle into that good night
> Old age should burn and rave at close
> of day
> Rage, rage against the dying of the
> light.

As I recall, he wrote these words when his father was dying. I don't mean to pursue a simplistic interpretation. They warrant a fuller probing if only as an exploration of the father-son relationship. It's certainly a plea from a young man full of life and promise to fight death. But as a mere instruction—"rage, rage against the dying of the light"—then I'm glad Dylan wasn't my kid. Near journey's end there is no room for rage and the frustration it leads to in the face of the realities of diminishment. Rather than the futility of rage, I know I must find worth in waiting, waiting as a spiritual practice, waiting that will perhaps offer me a window on God's love, waiting for an already sowed seed to root and sprout. Perhaps this is the experience of the mystics who wait for an encounter with God.

The possibilities inherent in the notion of a seed already sown internally intrigues me, a kind of pregnancy of old age.

The passivity of waiting may seem a strange spiritual practice, but French philosopher and resistance fighter Simone Weil tells us that "waiting patiently in expectation is the foundation of the spiritual life."

In a wonderful talk he recorded many years ago, Henri Nouwen broke open the spirituality of waiting. He said: "People who wait have received a promise that allows them to wait. They have received something that is at work in them, like a seed that has started to grow."

He points out that in the beginning of Luke's Gospel, Zechariah and Elizabeth, Mary, and Simeon and Anna, all wait with this sense of promise, with a seed in their hearts. Zechariah waits for the news that Elizabeth will bear him a son; the youthful, unmarried Mary awaits the news that she is to "conceive and bear a son. . . . He will be great and will be called the Son of the Most High." Simeon and Anna wait in the Temple to hold the Messiah at the Presentation. This is more than wish fulfillment. They wait for something that, in Nouwen's words, is "far beyond their own imaginings." They are all aware of the possibility of a seed but unaware of how it might bloom.

We can look further in the Gospels for an understanding of waiting.

The Anglican priest W. H. Vanstone points out that in the Gospel of Mark, Jesus is the subject, not the object, even when his enemies attack him. Jesus is active. That is, until he is handed over in the garden. His life then shifts from the active to the passive. "It is now all about what is done to him, not what he did. . . . His inner state becomes silent." He waits on the inevitable will of his Father.

In John the transition happens at the Last Supper when Jesus says that his work is done. "The activity of the day yields to the passivity of the night, and working becomes waiting," writes Vanstone.

A grand friend visited recently. It had been seven years since we were last together. Much had changed. Now eighty-four, Mary has been limited by arterial fibrillation, lupus, and diabetes. A noted biographer (John

Paul II, Lech Walesa, the Dalai Lama), author of a half-dozen books on other subjects, and an interviewer for the BBC's Radio Four, she is now dependent on walking sticks or a wheelchair. Her hands are withering, reducing touch-typing to the two-finger hunt and peck, to lifting a drinking glass with both hands. Yet, accompanied by her son, she got onto a plane for a transatlantic journey to a memorial service for an old friend and patron and several days with Sue and me.

I sat with this friend pained by isolation from the world she once chronicled intimately. Her sense of diminished worth was palpable, yielding only slowly to the encouragement of friends and the love of family. She has not found it easy to move from activity to passivity, from engagement to waiting. Nor will most of us.

She says, however, that in waiting she finds consolation. And in her waiting she remains a loved presence among family and friends. She prays, not often successfully. "I don't contemplate well. I never have." To be with her at this time of her life, to feel her deep friendship, enriched me once again. From her I learned that one day I might have to learn to wait with grace. I was struck by how hard this waiting is, how hard it will be to move from activity to passivity.

As a young woman Mary was, in her words, "blown away" by the writings of French paleontologist Pierre

Teilhard de Chardin. Now, in days that seem barren in comparison with the days of her accomplishments, she returns to him for sustenance, praying as Teilhard prays:

> When the signs of age begin to mark
> my body
> (and still more when they touch my
> mind);
> when the ill that is to diminish me or
> carry me off
> strikes from without or is born within
> me . . .
> O God, grant that I may understand
> that it is you . . .
> who are painfully parting the fibers of
> my being
> in order to penetrate to the very mar-
> row
> of my substance and bear me away
> within yourself.

"And bear me away within yourself." What a promise to ponder. What a beautiful image to wait with—one day we will become one with God.